The Pacific Ocean

MANAGING EDITORS
Amy Bauman
Barbara J. Behm

CONTENT EDITORS
Amanda Barrickman
James I. Clark
Patricia Lantier
Charles P. Milne, Jr.
Katherine C. Noonan
Christine Snyder
Gary Turbak
William M. Vogt
Denise A. Wenger
Harold L. Willis
John Wolf

ASSISTANT EDITORS
Ann Angel
Michelle Dambeck
Barbara Murray
Renee Prink
Andrea J. Schneider

INDEXER
James I. Clark

ART/PRODUCTION
Suzanne Beck, Art Director
Andrew Rupniewski, Production Manager
Eileen Rickey, Typesetter

Library of Congress Number: 88-18336

Library of Congress Cataloging-in-Publication Data

Bottoni, Luciana, 1952-
    [Oceano Pacifico. English]
    The Pacific Ocean / Luciana Bottoni, Valeria Lucini,
Renato Massa.

    — (World nature encyclopedia)
    Translation of: Oceano Pacifico.
    Includes index.
    Summary: Examines plant and animal life found in the
Pacific Ocean.
    1. Marine ecology—Pacific Ocean—Juvenile literature.
2. Marine biology—Pacific Ocean—Juvenile literature.
[1. Marine ecology—Pacific Ocean.   2. Marine biology—
Pacific Ocean.   3. Pacific Ocean. 4. Ecology.]   I. Lucini,
Valeria.   II. Massa, Renato. III. Title.   IV. Series.
QH95.B6313   1988   574.5′.2636′09164—dc19   88-18336
ISBN 0-8172-3325-3

WORLD NATURE ENCYCLOPEDIA

The Pacific Ocean

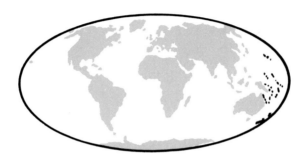

Luciana Bottoni
Valeria Lucini
Renato Massa

RAINTREE PUBLISHERS
Milwaukee

CONTENTS

INTRODUCTION

The world's largest ocean occupies about one-half of the earth. This ocean, which lies west of California and east of Japan and Australia, is the Pacific. Across this vast expanse of water, bits of land emerge almost like floating rafts. Some are large; some are small. But of the thousands of pieces of land that emerge here and there in the ocean, no two are exactly the same.

The islands north of Australia (New Guinea, the Moluccas, New Britain, New Ireland, Bismarck, and the Solomon Islands) are similar in many ways to Australia. At the same time, they have many characteristics of their own. They also have many characteristics in common with Indonesia. To the southwest, New Zealand is a unique set of islands. It has very little in common with Australia or with any other part of the world. To the east and northeast, finally, New Caledonia, the Fiji Islands, Samoa, and other islands of South Melanesia and Polynesia, all the way to

Tahiti and Hawaii, are like stepping stones across the ocean from Australia to America.

The islands are also a kind of beautiful "prison" for the plants and animals that have ended up there. They will always be full of biological surprises and many unique circumstances that cannot be reproduced anywhere else. As one goes farther and farther onto the ocean, the islands are also more and more isolated from the rest of the world.

This book offers a look at the natural history of New Zealand and the main islands of the Pacific, starting with New Caledonia and moving toward the east, north, and northeast, toward Micronesia, Polynesia, and southern Melanesia. New Guinea and the nearby islands of northern Melanesia are set aside. Because of their size, similarities, and the special richness of their mountain and forest habitats, they are a world unto themselves. They are worth studying in more detail by themselves in another volume.

THE PACIFIC OCEAN

The first European to look upon the vast blue expanse of the Pacific was Vasco Nunez de Balboa in 1513. But even after Balboa's discovery, it was a long time before anyone realized that the Pacific was the largest ocean on earth. The Pacific Ocean, which is also larger than any land mass on earth, covers one-third of the planet's surface. Its water makes up one-half of all the world's water.

Geophysical Characteristics

The Pacific Ocean has distinct geographical boundaries. To the east, the boundaries are North and South America. To the west, they are Asia and Australia. To the north, the ocean is bounded by the Bering Strait. To the south, its waters mix with those of the Indian and Atlantic oceans. Within these boundaries, the entire area of the Pacific is about 70 million square miles (180 million square kilometers), of which almost 8 million sq. miles (20 million sq. km) are part of smaller seas: the Bering Sea, the Sea of Okhotsk, the Sea of Japan, the Chinese Sea, the Philippine Sea, and the Coral Sea. All of these smaller seas are on the western side. On the eastern side, the only smaller sea within the Pacific Ocean is the Gulf of California. Thus, there is a noticeable difference between the two sides of the ocean. The western side is very rich with islands, peninsulas, and archipelagoes, which are groups of islands. The eastern side, on the other hand, has smooth coastlines and very few islands.

The physical, chemical, and dynamic characteristics of the ocean waters determine the establishment and growth of different biological communities. Even small changes in these characteristics can have an enormous influence on the communities' life forms and their interrelationships.

A very important characteristic of the water of this huge ocean is the average temperature at its surface, which is just a little warmer in the Northern Hemisphere than in the Southern Hemisphere. The warmest average temperature, which is about 82° Fahrenheit (28° Celsius), is found in a large band between the northern coast of Australia and the southern coast of Japan. This band runs along the equator halfway between Asia and North America.

Along the North American coast, the temperatures are lower, except for a small area between the Gulf of California and the Isthmus of Panama. In this area, the temperature averages 86° to 90°F (30° to 32°C). The water of this region, however, does not generally mix with the rest of the ocean

Preceding pages: This atoll, made of coral reef in Polynesia, is located between Tahiti and the Fiji Islands. This type of atoll is called a "coralline atoll."

Opposite page: A high wave breaks against the solidified lava coast of Easter Island.

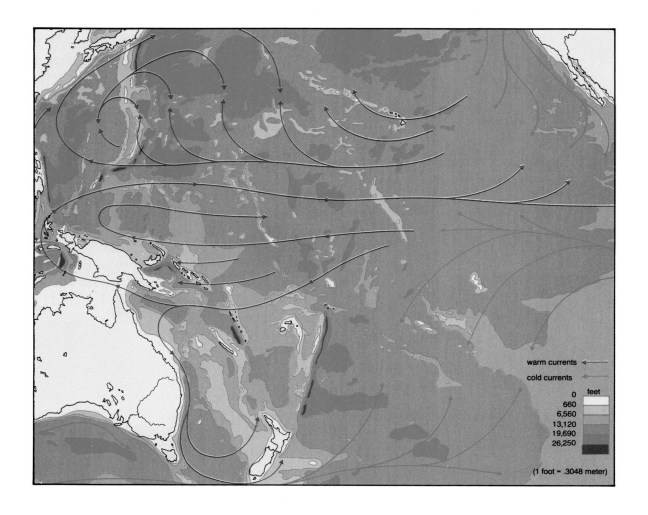

This diagram shows the main currents of the Pacific and its depths. The largest ocean in the world is characterized by an active circulation of both cold and warm waters. This circulation sometimes causes great variations of average temperatures on land. The depths here are the deepest on the planet, with some trenches reaching more than 36,089 feet (11,000 m).

warm currents
cold currents

	feet
0	
660	
6,560	
13,120	
19,690	
26,250	

(1 foot = .3048 meter)

water. As a result, the sun's rays have a greater warming effect on the water here than on waters that circulate with the ocean currents.

In the South Pacific, these differences in temperature are even more noticeable. The direction of the southern currents is exactly the opposite of the direction of the northern ones. In addition, the currents in the South Pacific are affected by the Antarctic Current. This current, which moves along the coast of South America, splits into two different branches. One moves around Cape Horn and travels toward the Atlantic. The other, the Humboldt Current, moves up the coasts of Chile and Peru.

The most important characteristic of the Humboldt Current is the low temperature of its water. It is generally between 50° and 59°F (10° to 15°C), which is much lower

Above: This diagram shows the formation of a tsunami. The wave is caused by earthquake activity and gets higher and higher as it moves.

Below: This map examines the speed of a spreading tidal wave. From its point of origin near the South American coast, a powerful tsunami can reach the islands in the middle of the Pacific in about fourteen hours.

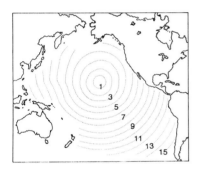

than the temperature of the waters or air around it. In addition, its waters have a lower level of salinity, or saltiness, than the waters off the coast. It is also very rich in the microscopic plants, called "diatoms," that give it an intense green color.

About 65 percent of the Pacific Ocean has a depth between 13,000 and 20,000 feet (4,000 to 6,000 meters). This is much greater than the Atlantic, where such depths are found only in 46 percent of its area.

In addition, the Atlantic's sediment layer is a couple of miles thick. This sediment layer is composed of soil, gravel, sand, and other matter that settles to the bottom of the ocean. In the Pacific, this layer is much thinner, ranging from 650 to 1,300 feet (200 to 400 m) thick. This difference in sediment thicknesses gave rise to different theories. The most widely accepted of these theories proposes that the sediment in the Pacific undergoes greater erosion than the sediment in the Atlantic. Erosion causes the heaviest mineral elements to settle to the very bottom of the sediment. This explains why these elements appear in the deepest strata, or layers. There, the mineral elements are changed into other types of rocks. This change is caused by physical forces, such as pressure and heat, and chemical reactions that occur when the rocks come into contact with the thick, molten rock called "magma."

Tidal Waves and Typhoons

The name *Pacific*, which means "peaceful," was given to the ocean by the explorer Ferdinand Magellan. He came upon it in 1520, when his ships escaped a storm in the strait which now bears his name (the Magellan Strait). Contrary to its name, this ocean is rougher and stormier than all other oceans. Often the Pacific has severe storms and typhoons that can cause great damage.

Only in the Pacific, as a matter of fact, do the famous tidal waves occur, bringing death and destruction to the coasts. The "tsunami," as it is called in Japanese, is an isolated wave that looks like a wall of water. This wave is unusual for two reasons. First, it is not preceded or followed by other waves. Second, a tsunami can move a great amount of water. An object floating on the crest, in fact, is pushed forward just as it would be in a river. The source of this type of wave is without a doubt from seismic activity.

The Pacific is literally surrounded by a ring of volcanoes and seismic zones that are powerful sources of under-

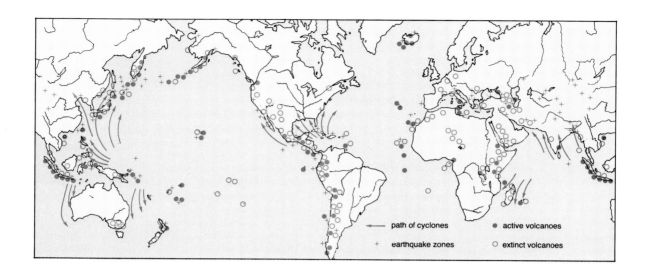

path of cyclones   ● active volcanoes

+ earthquake zones   ○ extinct volcanoes

water earthquakes. This "Ring of Fire" begins in New Zealand, follows along the Tonga Islands, New Guinea, the Philippines, Japan, Kamchatka, and the Aleutian Islands, and then runs down the American coasts to the Peruvian and Chilean volcanoes. Just a little shifting of the earth is all that is needed for a tidal wave to begin. Once it has formed, it does not die out completely until it has reached land.

The speed of this wave is usually very fast. One of the most famous tidal waves that hit Hawaii in 1946 was about 66 feet (20 m) high. It caused the death of hundreds of people and millions of dollars' worth of damage. Seismologists, or people who study earthquakes, discovered that after the wave originated near the Aleutian Islands, it reached Hawaii in less than six hours. It traveled almost 2,500 miles (4,000 km) at an average speed of 430 to 500 miles (700 to 800 km) per hour.

Tidal waves are not the only catastrophies that occur in the Pacific Ocean. Another natural phenomenon with terrible consequences is that of cyclone winds. These winds, called "typhoons," reach a force of hundreds of miles per hour. These winds are capable of raising monstrous waves. Typhoons begin with the action of heat on the ocean's surface near the equator, which causes large masses of warm, humid air to rise in the atmosphere. As the air rises, it cools, and its moisture condenses, releasing its heat in a process which creates wind. A typhoon keeps its force for a long time over the water.

Formation and Structure

The origin of the Pacific Ocean can be traced to the breaking up of the supercontinent called "Pangaea." This occurred during the Mesozoic era, a period of time lasting from 230 million to 65 million years ago. The separation of the continents and the formation of the other oceans occurred at about the same time. The land masses drifted after their separation from larger continents.

The supercontinent Pangaea then separated into two smaller continents. The northern continent is now called "Laurasia," and the southern one is known as "Gondwanaland." The evolution of Gondwanaland was very important to the origin of the Pacific. Gondwanaland later broke apart, resulting in the formation of India. Further fractures of Gondwanaland brought about a series of movements that caused the formation of the islands of Australia and Antarctica. India continued to drift toward the north, while Austra-

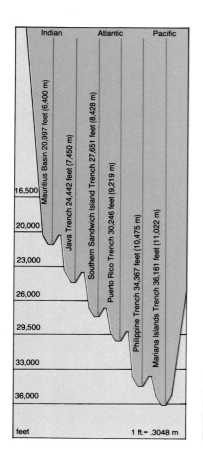

Ocean trenches in the three great oceans of the earth can reach tremendous depths. The Pacific Ocean is not only the largest, but also the deepest ocean. Some of its trenches are more than 36,000 feet (11,000 m) deep. The deepest trenches of the Atlantic Ocean are slightly more than 29,527 feet (9,000 m) deep. Those of the Indian Ocean are less than 25,000 feet (7,500 m) deep.

lia and Antarctica moved toward the south. This movement continues even today.

These geologic events were confirmed by a study of the ocean depths. There, scientists have found underwater mountain chains separated by a deep central fault, or crack. This fault continues to spread apart, leaving an empty space that is then filled with magma which flows out from the fracture's depths. Once the magma reaches the surface, it solidifies into a rock formation on the ocean bottom. This same type of activity caused the breakup of the Pangaea supercontinent and formed the oceans.

These geological changes left a number of traces that are evident today. On the bottom of the Pacific off the Asian coasts, there are various trenches that range from 16,000 to 36,000 feet (5,000 to 11,000 m). As mentioned previously, the Pacific is characterized by intense seismic activity that is of great interest to scientists. Earthquakes often originate in a sloping zone that slips into a trench beneath the continental slope. Following these observations, scientists have come to the theory that where ocean trenches are formed, the earth's crust wears away. That is, the dense oceanic crust sinks lower than the continental crust. This phenomenon is called "subduction." The crust continues to form while the ridge wears away right along the edges of the Pacific.

In addition, it should be noted that where these trenches exist, chains of islands of volcanic origin are always present. They, too, are probably formed by subduction. The slipping of the oceanic crust beneath the continental crust creates heat because of friction. The heat causes the earth's crust to become partially liquified, or molten. Because of the strong pressure and high temperature, the molten rock tends to rise, forming volcanic islands.

Formation of the Islands

The Pacific islands, however, are not all of volcanic origin. Some are the remains of continents. Others, called "coralline islands," are made of coral.

New Zealand is one of the best examples of the islands that are the remains of continents. These islands were once part of a much greater earthly mass. Some became islands when they broke off and drifted away from the continent. Others formed when the land areas connecting them to the continent sank. Further evidence of the continental origin of these islands is the existence of underwater chains that link them to the closest continents. The most convincing proof

A cross section of a coral atoll shows a layer of living corals growing on the remains of dead corals (A and B). The bottom layer of dead corals grew on top of volcanic rock many years ago (C). In the lower illustration, several coral-producing "polyps" can be seen. These animals are very simple organisms. They have cylindrical bodies and mouths surrounded by tentacles.

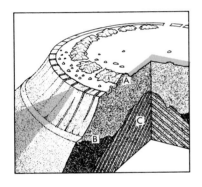

comes from a geological comparison of the soil.

The volcanic and coralline islands are concentrated in the western and central zones of the Pacific. As noted earlier, the Pacific Ocean is known for its "Ring of Fire." It holds the record among the oceans for active volcanoes; even the ocean is strewn with volcanic peaks. Some of them are simply undulations, or little ripples, in the ocean floor. Others are hundreds or thousands of feet high. The accumulation of lava in some cases was great enough to make them visible above the water's surface. These volcanic peaks are subject to erosion by waves and other factors. For such reasons, some islands that are formed this way have a very brief existence. In other cases, the islands are able to withstand these natural forces.

Finally, the warm waters of the Pacific also have some nonvolcanic chains of islands. These ring-shaped islands barely rise above the water's surface. Called "atolls," these islands are bordered with white beaches lush with palm trees. These islands are made of coral, or of the polyps that make up a coral reef. Polyps are little animals that live in colonies. They look like fragile, gelatinlike flowers and have numerous sharp tentacles. Every year, the polyps deposit an additional layer of limestone on the existing layers. The limestone structure can be produced only in waters with a temperature greater than 73°F (23°C). For this reason, all of the atolls are found in the western section of the Pacific in a band 30 degrees north and south of the equator.

Charles Darwin, the English naturalist, was the first to propose that the great atolls began with the formation of smaller reefs along the coastlines of old eroded volcanic islands. After the reef formed, the central mass of the island sank at a rate that allowed a balance between the sinking land and the growing coral. However, Darwin could not prove his hypothesis. Even today, the reason for the sinking is unknown.

NEW ZEALAND

The Pacific Ocean evokes visions of flat, white atolls and tropical islands covered with coconut palms and surrounded by emerald green waters. For the most part, this dreamy image is true. But, like all stereotypes, it is far from being the only reality of this great expanse of water that covers such a large part of the planet.

A "Different" Archipelago

New Zealand is an archipelago, or chain of islands, located about 1,243 miles (2,000 km) southeast of Australia. This country is grouped around two large islands that together look like an upside-down boot. The islands of New Zealand cover about 103,448 sq. miles (268,000 sq. km) from about 34 to 48 degrees latitude south. New Zealand is a land of spectacular mountains, deep fiords, immense glaciers, and rich temperate and subtropical forests. A fragment of ancient continents, this land's native inhabitants provide the proof of a very distant past. Its unique isolation and the results of its relatively recent contact with humans are also proof of New Zealand's distant past.

The Discovery of New Zealand

The discovery of the two large islands that make up New Zealand is attributed to the very capable Polynesian navigators. These Polynesian sailors must have known about the islands' existence for a long time because of the halo of clouds that crowns them, visible even from far away.

This halo of clouds is so consistent that these lands are also called "the misty islands" or "the land of fog." The fog is formed when moisture condenses as it is forced to rise along the mountain slopes. The other islands are too low to undergo this phenomenon.

New Zealand was one of the last great land areas to be settled by humans. Credit is given to the great Polynesian explorer Kupe for the discovery of New Zealand. Kupe landed on the islands around A.D. 1000. According to legend, Kupe landed on the new land by accident. Legend has it, in fact, that he was drawn there by a giant octopus he had harpooned. Upon his return to the island of Hawaiki—probably present-day Tahiti—he told the story of a wonderful faraway land. According to the legend, that is why many inhabitants of the Society Islands sailed for the places of which Kupe had spoken. After sailing about two thousand miles, these sailors reached the island they called *Aotearoa*, which, in the Maori language, means "the land of the

Opposite page: Doubtful Sound, a fiord of glacial origin, is found on the South Island. New Zealand has the nickname "Switzerland of the South Pacific" because of its spectacular mountains.

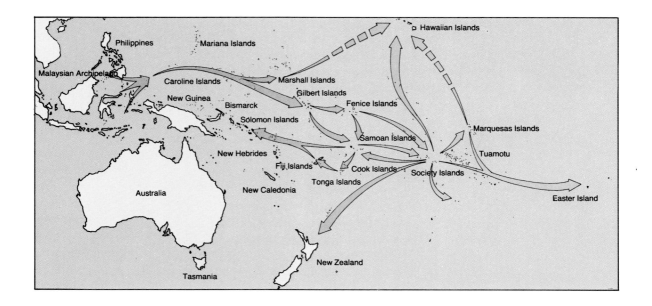

This diagram shows the migration of Polynesians in the Pacific Ocean. Their route was similar to that of many animals. They left the easternmost islands of Asia and moved across the open sea in small sturdy boats. They went from one island to another and populated even the most remote and unknown corners of the ocean. New Zealand remained isolated for a very long time. The first human beings reached it in relatively recent times and greatly modified the environment even before the first Europeans arrived. (see map)

long, white cloud."

According to the most recent archaeological excavations, the human presence in New Zealand came about in approximately A.D. 600 to 1200. Of course, the origin of the people who arrived by boat must be researched in eastern Polynesia, among the archipelagoes of Hawaii, the Marquesas Islands, the Society Islands, and the Cook Islands. Even so, it is impossible to say which of these was their homeland, just as it is not known if they settled there in one migration or many.

Although these primitive people were involved in agriculture (they grew sweet potatoes, itaro, squash, and so on), they lived mostly from fishing and hunting. Their favorite prey was the moa, a giant running bird that became extinct between A.D. 1000 and 1350. After the moa became extinct, the Maoris, as these people were called, continued to fish and trap many wild birds, even though most of their food came from fern roots. Gathering the ferns pushed them farther and farther into the interior of the island. The Maori population lived undisturbed and isolated until 1642, when the Danish explorer Abel Tasman drove them back to the sea. Another 127 years of "solitude" passed before they were forced to surrender to James Cook and his men. The colonization by the Europeans followed. Besides radically changing the flora, or plant life, and fauna, or animal life, this colonization caused the downfall of the Maori society.

A view of Mount Tasman and the Fox Glacier in Westland National Park is shown. Spectacular mountains like this are common in New Zealand. Their environments have a large number of ecological niches in which a great number of plants and animals are able to live.

Physical Aspects

New Zealand is made up of the North Island and the South Island, which are separated by Cook Strait. Despite the fact that it is located 1,240 miles (2,000 km) southeast of Australia, it is without a doubt the remains of a continent. Studies of the soil reveal this fact. Most of the rocks are sedimentary. This fact indicates the islands' connection to continental masses in times past. The short New Zealand streams would never have been able to leave such a great accumulation of sediment. In addition, the flora and fauna of the two islands form an ecosystem, or ecological system, completely different from any other. On the one hand, rather primitive species have survived, while on the other hand, entire groups of more recent species are completely missing. This indicates a separation from the continental masses to which it was connected a long time ago.

New Zealand has various types of landscapes. Moun-

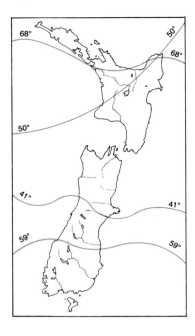

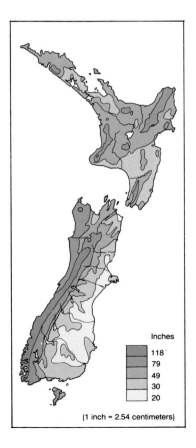

Inches

118
79
49
30
20

(1 inch = 2.54 centimeters)

tain chains alternate with valleys and plains. There are numerous glaciers and fiords as well as volcanoes and geysers which shoot out columns of hot water in the air. These features are evidence of volcanic activity that occurred during the formation of the islands.

The climate is typically temperate. It is warmer in the north and cooler in the south because of the mountains that hold the mist as it rolls in from the sea. Precipitation is common, especially in the winter months (from May to October). This favors the growth of an abundant vegetation. New Zealand still has large areas of original forests, even though many trees have been cut down or destroyed by fire to make way for farming.

The antarctic beech forest is found in the southwestern region, where rainfall is heavy. This forest has five different species of beech trees: silver, mountain, black, red, and hard. Toward the center is a forest of podocarp trees with a rich undergrowth. The obvious remains of a subtropical forest are found in the northwestern part, which is warmer. The giant trees of the *Agathis* genus are most common here.

With an increase in elevation, the forest is replaced by steppes and meadows, where nonwoody plants are more common. Grasses and mosses are the most common plants of the higher elevation. These plant forms are typical of the high peaks of the South Island. In fact, this is about the only place they grow.

The high peaks, glaciers, and icy mountain lakes of the South Island reminded European colonists of the Alps. They nicknamed the island "the Switzerland of the South Pacific." The coasts are rugged and pierced by deep fiords. The coasts of the North Island, on the other hand, have good ports, bays, and harbors. The interior of the South Island is also very different from the interior of the North Island. The South Island has dense antarctic beech forests. These are rare on the North Island, which is covered with tree ferns and kauri pine trees. The two islands of New Zealand must have struck European colonists as a beautiful combination of the various landscapes of their own continent.

The North Island

The shores of the North Island are covered by coastal shrubs. These are scattered spiny palms and low pines, clumps of Nikau palms and rata trees. The rata trees are called "Christmas trees" in New Zealand because their red flowers are the most splendid in December.

Opposite page: These maps show maximum temperature and rainfall in New Zealand. *(Top):* the red shows the average daily variation in temperature in July. The blue shows the average daily variation in temperature in January. *(Bottom):* a gradual change in color marks the annual precipitation levels on the two islands.

Right: A group of palm trees lines the shore of an island in the Pacific. The palms are monocotyledons, which means that they have one seed leaf. They are tropical plants with single leaves grouped together in a tuft at the top. Their fruit resembles pineapples. Like pineapples, they have leaf bracts that resemble other parts of flowers. Many years ago, the plants of the palm family were much more common. They are distributed throughout the tropical regions of Africa, Asia, Australia, and Polynesia, including Hawaii.

At one time, there were many different species of the unusual moa birds that lived only in New Zealand. All of them became extinct by the seventeenth century due to hunting by the Maori people.

The island's interior was once covered by tall, lush forests of kauri pines and tree ferns together with a rich undergrowth of bushes. Because of their remarkable size and the quality of their wood, the kauri pines were widely used for lumber. This wood was especially well suited for shipbuilding. So many trees were cut down for this purpose that of the 3,088 sq. miles (8,000 sq. km) once covered by forest, only 39 sq. miles (100 sq. km) remain today.

In the kauri pine forest of Waipona, north of Auckland, there are still many examples of these hundred-year-old kauri pines. They rise up above the dense subtropical jungle, their trunks wrapped with vines and climbing plants. Many other species are characteristic of this forest. *Pinus rimus* is a pine tree with graceful little hanging branches. It supplies a large amount of the wood used for building in New Zealand.

New Zealand's original plant life has some similarities with the plant life of the mountains of New Guinea and New Caledonia. These two islands are also fragments of continents. However, a comparison with the plant life of Australia is also impossible. Only the orchids, ferns, and plants with wind-borne seeds, or spores, are similar in both Australia and New Zealand. The eucalyptus trees and reeds, which are common in Australia, are completely absent in New Zealand, except for those introduced in recent years.

Moas

When the first Polynesians landed on New Zealand about one thousand years ago, they discovered one of the earth's most unusual animal species, the moas. These giant plant-eating birds reached a height of 10 to 13 feet (3 to 4 m). The moas roamed the plains of New Zealand in much the same way as the antelope roam the African savanna today, moving in herds as they search for food.

Charles Darwin studied the many species of birds and insects that had lost the use of their wings in New Zealand. According to the famous naturalist, the ability to fly was no longer beneficial in an environment constantly battered by strong winds. The ancestors of the moas, who had flown to the area, found numerous ecological niches that plant-eating mammals might have filled in continental communities. In the course of evolution, these birds adapted easily to their new environment. Since there were no other mammals, there was no competition for food. The birds evolved into numerous species and grew steadily in size over the

The small frogs of the *Leiopelma* genus do not seem unusual at first glance. Only a careful examination of their internal anatomy reveals their descendence from ancient amphibians. These frogs left the water to inhabit a land environment between 135 and 180 million years ago. They were able to survive because there were few competing animals in the isolated environments of New Zealand.

years until they reached the size of the most common plant-eating mammals. Among present-day animals, only the giraffe and the African elephant are taller than the now-extinct moas.

The first traces that prove the existence of the moas were discovered in the nineteenth century. Based on fossil evidence, Sir Richard Owen, an English paleontologist (a scientist who studies fossils), concluded in 1843 that many species of moas had existed. None of these had a bone structure similar to that of the earlier winged moas. In later excavations, many perfectly preserved skeletons were uncovered. In these excavations, an egg of amazing size was discovered. It measured 7 by 5 inches (17 by 12 centimeters). In addition, the remains of a moa's last meal were found. The meal consisted of seeds, twigs, coarse grass, leaves, and fruit.

The large species of moas became extinct, or died out, around the fourteenth century. The smaller species, which lived on the South Island, disappeared around the seventeenth century. It is certain that their extinction was caused by over-hunting. The early Maoris were great hunters of this bird and are sometimes called the "moa hunters." The discovery of bones and moa eggs near the ruins of their campfires is proof of this fact.

Living Fossils

The primitive frogs and the tuatara reptiles provide evidence that New Zealand and Australia or Antarctica were once united. The islands of these two countries separated in the Jurassic period, which lasted from 180 million to 135 million years ago. Since the above animals are found in both New Zealand and Australia, it is likely that New Zealand separated from Australia during that period. The frogs would not have been able to swim to New Zealand from Australia after the separation, since they cannot survive the salinity of the seawater. The tuatara reptiles became extinct on the continents due to the appearance of new competing species of reptiles, birds, and mammals during the Jurassic period. The existence of the tuatara reptiles in New Zealand proves that it was already isolated before the appearance of the competing animals on the continents.

The Archey frog, the Hochstetter frog, and the Hamilton frog are all species of the *Leiopelma* genus. These frogs are characterized by a primitive type of backbone and male reproductive organs. In the adult stage, these frogs have

23

Although they look like the true lizards, the tuatara reptiles are actually completely different. They are part of a different order that became extinct in other parts of the world between 135 and 180 million years ago. At the beginning of the last century, the tuatara reptiles were numerous throughout New Zealand. However, after the European settlement, dogs, cats, and pigs killed them off almost everywhere. They have survived in only thirteen islands that have no domesticated predators.

traces of tail muscles, which are another primitive feature. They live near mountain streams and grow only about 2 inches (5 cm) in length. Because of their small size, they can use the holes dug by insects as safe hiding places.

These frogs are poor swimmers and spend most of their lives out of water. Unlike most other frogs, they do not need water to reproduce. When the eggs of these frogs hatch, the little frogs are already completely developed. Therefore, they do not have a tadpole stage that requires water. The newly hatched young differ from the adult frog only by the presence of a long tail. The tail enables the young frog to breathe until its lungs are completely developed. When the young frogs become adults, the tail disappears, but some traces of the tail muscle remain.

Primitive traits are even more evident in the tuatara reptiles. Called "living fossils," these animals are the best example of New Zealand's isolation. The tuatara is the only species of its order that managed to survive. The other animals of this reptile order living in other parts of the world became extinct during the Jurassic period. The tuatara,

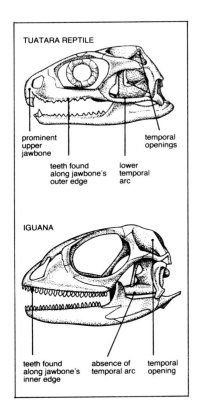

TUATARA REPTILE

prominent
upper
jawbone

temporal
openings

teeth found
along jawbone's
outer edge

lower
temporal
arc

IGUANA

teeth found
along jawbone's
inner edge

absence of
temporal arc

temporal
opening

The skull of the tuatara reptile *(above)* differs from that of the lizards *(below, that of the iguana)* in various ways. The tuatara reptile has a beaklike structure, two distinct temporal openings instead of just one, and teeth located along the edge of the lower and upper jawbones. The teeth are not all alike. There are two wedge-shaped teeth that are much larger than the others located on the lower jaw.

which dates back to the time of the dinosaurs, is about 18 inches (45 cm) long and looks like a giant lizard. It is dark gray and has a crest that extends all along the back, beginning at the back of the head. The crest is similar to that of many lizards and iguanas. The tuatara is also characterized by a "third eye."

The third eye is a feature commonly found in fossils of many extinct vertebrates (animals with backbones). It is the pineal eye, which is less developed than the other two, but with a retina and a lens. This eye is found in a more basic form in numerous species of lizards, and it is very important for cold-blooded animals. The pineal eye's sensitivity to light enables the animal to regulate its exposure to the sun. The temperature of a cold-blooded animal, such as a reptile, changes with the environment's temperature. The third eye warns the animal to take shelter from extreme heat.

The tuatara has a primitive type of backbone, like that of fish and the frogs of the *Leiopelma* genus. Its metabolism, which is the sum of its physical and chemical life processes, is the slowest among the vertebrate animals. It functions even at temperatures as low as 52°F (11°C). Nevertheless, the tuataras go into hibernation, or become inactive, from autumn to spring.

Kiwis

The kiwi is the national symbol of New Zealand. At first glance, this bird seems related to ostriches, rheas, and emus, all of which are flightless running birds. These birds are so similar that in the past zoologists classified them in just one group. Now it seems that these different land birds have no common ancestor at all. Their resemblance to each other is simply due to an unusual combination of events.

The striped kiwi lives on the North Island, while two different species, the great spotted kiwi and the little spotted kiwi, live on the South Island. These birds also have several subspecies. Kiwis live in forests having a dense undergrowth. They are nocturnal birds which means they are active at night.

These strange birds have managed to survive in spite of environmental changes and the introduction of nonnative predators. Their tapered bodies are covered with long, odd feathers that are coarse and frayed. The feathers covering the crude wings are of the same type as the feathers covering the rest of the body, while other birds have a different, special type of feather for their wings.

A kiwi is seen with its huge egg. The eggs of this bird weigh about one-sixth of the weight of the adult bird. The symbol of New Zealand, these unique nocturnal land birds are easy to spot in the wild. Nevertheless, it is not true that they are endangered species, as some zoologists reported several years ago.

Another difference between the kiwi and other birds is the kiwi's lack of a tail. These running birds have short, powerful legs and four strong claws. Their beaks are long and flexible, and the lower part is shorter than the upper part. The nostrils are on the tip of the upper beak. In other birds, nostrils are found at the beak's base. The kiwi's unusual beak, together with its habit of digging with its beak to find underground food, led zoologists to believe that these birds have a very good sense of smell. This was confirmed by research conducted by a zoologist of the University of California. The researcher found that the kiwi can smell

certain substances placed as deep as 10 inches (25 cm) in the ground. Its sense of hearing is also very developed. The kiwi's eyes, however, are very small, and it has poor vision, as do most nocturnal animals.

During the rainy season, the kiwi feeds on small invertebrates (animals lacking a backbone). It uses its sense of smell to detect earthworms and then pulls them out of the ground with the tip of its long beak. It also pulls small insects from tree trunks just as woodpeckers do. To do this, it probably uses its sense of hearing, which enables it to pick up vibrations from its hidden prey. During the summer, when the earth is dry, the kiwis become herbivores, or plant-eaters. They feed mostly on leaves and fruit that drop to the ground in this season.

Because of their nocturnal habits, all species of kiwi are difficult to observe. Therefore, little is known about their behavior patterns. It is known that the male tends the eggs laid by the female in a simple hole dug in the ground. This is true of other flightless birds as well. The female never lays more than two eggs in any mating season, and they are large. The female of the striped kiwi, for example, weighs about 7 pounds (3 kilograms). It lays an egg that weighs about 1 pound (0.5 kg). In relation to their body weight, kiwis lay the largest eggs of all the birds in the world. Less than three months after they are laid, the eggs hatch and the chicks are cared for by the male.

Marsh Birds

Several species of rails and gallinules living in New Zealand have lost the ability to fly. This is a result of the islands' favorable living conditions as well as the lack of predators. Once a species has lost its ability to fly, it is unlikely that it will regain it. Losing this ability can be dangerous for a bird species. Obviously it will not be able to fly away from predators that might be introduced, and the remains of various forms of extinct rails and gallinules have been found in New Zealand. The takahe and the weka are the only remaining species found in New Zealand. The takahe looks like a huge sultan chicken and is about 2 feet, (63 cm) long. It lives in the mountain zones of the South Island in grasslands and low underbrush. It feeds on every type of plant, especially on their seeds. The weka is similar to a water rail and inhabits the North Island.

The takahe spends most of its time searching for small vertebrates and insects among spiny shrubs. These make up

Penguins of New Zealand include *(from top to bottom, left to right:)* the yellow-eyed penguin, the blue penguin, the royal penguin, and the crested penguin.

a large part of its diet. Takahes were thought to be extinct at one time, but some were discovered in 1948 in a glacial valley high in the New Zealand Alps. Not much is known about the takahe, except that the female lays only two eggs and can nest twice in one mating season. The fact that it can nest twice in one season, however, has not increased the population of tahakes. Due to the extensive hunting of this bird by newly introduced predators, it is now an endangered species.

The Parakeets of New Zealand

Four different species of parakeets are found in New Zealand. For the most part, they all inhabit the same area. They are compatible because the size of their beaks keeps them from competing for the same kind of food.

These crested parakeets all belong to the same genus. They are greenish on top, yellowish underneath, and light blue on their wing feathers. Only their heads have different colors. The red-headed parakeets are the most widespread and live on the surrounding islands. The yellow-headed parakeets are smaller and less common. The orange-headed parakeets live only in mountain zones. The fourth species (the Antipodes parakeet) is found only in the rocky, uninhabited islands off the southeastern coast of New Zealand.

The red-headed and the yellow-headed parakeets inhabit the same forests. They eat plant seeds, fruit, leaves, and recently, even farm plants. They often fly to the ground to feed. Unlike other parrots, they scratch around in search of small invertebrates, which enables them to survive in areas where the forests have been cut down. The other two species are much more specialized. The Antipodes parakeet has features that are more characteristic of an island bird. It is larger, lacks feathers, and cannot fly very well. These parakeets eat what little plant life there is on the islands. They also eat the remaining eggs and carcasses of penguins left behind after attacks of jaeger birds. The jaegers are seabirds that commonly attack colonies of penguins.

The Fireflies of Waitomo

On the North Island, a very special natural phenomenon can be seen in the caves of Waitomo. This is a well-known tourist site. The Waitomo River flows into the caves, which can be reached only by boat. Tourists visiting the caves are struck by the thousands of little "lanterns" that

A buttercup is found on the Cook Mountains in the Southern Alps of New Zealand. The flora of the high mountains of this faraway land in the Pacific has unique characteristics. They also have features that are very similar to those of the plants found in the other temperate mountain regions of the earth, such as the Eurasian and North American plants.

light up the entire ceiling.

These shining little lights are the countless tiny fireflies of Waitomo, which are just 0.5 inch (1.25 cm) long. They are not adult fireflies, but rather firefly larvae that live in the webs they spin. Thin, sticky strands hang from the webs, and the web strands serve as fishing lines. The larvae use them to catch little insects that come out of the water. Attracted by the light, the insects fly upward, where they are trapped by the sticky webs. Fireflies of the Northern Hemisphere, however, use their lights to attract mates.

The South Island

The South Island is divided into eastern and western sections by the high chain of the Southern Alps. These mountains extend along the entire length of the island from north to south. The elevations and shapes of the mountain peaks indicate that their rock formations are relatively recent. Like the European Alps, the Southern Alps are dotted with mountain lakes, created by glaciers, that extend

Milford Sound is one of many sounds found in New Zealand. The New Zealand sounds are valleys formed by glaciers of the Quaternary period (beginning about one million years ago) that were later filled by the sea. They stretch as far as 19 miles (30 km) into the interior of the mountain ranges. Milford Sound is the most accessible of all. The others, which are located on the southernmost coasts, are not often seen. They are not accessible by land, and the sea is constantly stormy. The New Zealand sounds were explored only in the second half of the last century.

along their slopes. The glaciers sometimes move down the slopes to elevations as low as 656 feet (200 m). Melting occurs at this elevation, as in the case of the Great Fox Glacier on Mount Tasman.

The great mountain chain causes the western clouds to drop their rain before passing over the mountains. This rain gives rise to the lush forests of the western coast. At the same time, the mountain ridge protects the eastern part of the island from the strong ocean winds and snows. Only some of the clouds pass to the eastern side of the mountains before dropping their rain. As a result, the eastern climate is milder and more favorable for the development of vast meadows.

Unusual plant species are found in the highest elevations above the treeline. The strange grass tree of the *Dracophyllum* genus, for example, has a thin, twisted trunk topped with a tuft of leaves similar to that of the pineapple. The sunken areas of the mountains are thickly covered with low-growing pine trees.

The most famous flower among the New Zealand mountain plants is the giant mountain buttercup. Its flower petals reach 2 inches (5 cm) in diameter. Snow daisies and Canterbury bells are often found near the giant buttercups.

At the northern end of the Southern Alps there are many short rivers which are noted for their spectacular gorges. A colony of white egrets lives on the banks of one of these rivers near Okarito. This Australian species colonized this area during the last century, roosting on the fronds of tree ferns in a dense forest. This habitat differs greatly from their original habitat in Australia, which was swampy with a few bare trees. Various species of migratory antarctic birds live near the mouths of these rivers, especially in the summer. These include the bar-tailed godwit, which has a white head, and two species of oystercatchers, the spotted and soot-black species.

The land of the fiords (which are narrow inlets of sea between cliffs or steep slopes) extends south of the Southern Alps. Its coast has deep inlets that rival the fiords of Norway for their beauty. Numerous red-beaked or black-beaked sea gulls and New Zealand tufted ducks can be found on the grassy peaks high above the sea. The land of the fiords also boasts the most extraordinary lakes on the island. Some of these lakes have deep branches that extend toward the interior across gorges and dense forests. Some actually look like fiords; hence the name "land of the fiords."

Opposite page: Typical birds of New Zealand include *(from left to right, and from top to bottom:)* New Zealand pigeon (in flight), New Zealand falcon (on top rock), kokako (on lower rock), Moreport owl (on bare branch), kea (in flight, near the top), and the giant petrel (bottom, in the distance), saddleback, tui, and kaka (on branches), red-headed parakeet (on a rock), kakapo (sitting in the foreground), weka, takahe, flycatchers, and spotted cormorant.

Among these lakes is Lake Wakatipu. It is 1,640 feet (500 m) deep and is located in territory that is difficult to reach. In fact, the road to the lake is 14 miles (22 km) long and has 480 curves, even though the distance from the lake to where the road begins is only 3,281 feet (1,000 m). According to Maori legend, the beauty of the lake is due to the fact that it was created by the supernatural powers of a great chief.

The banks of these lakes are lined with beech forests. The magnificent paradise goose lives in this habitat. The male has a black head and breast and a brick-red underside. In recent years, this goose has been introduced into the North Island as well, where it has successfully adapted to the new environment.

Bird Life of the South Island

The roughness of the terrain of the fiords has helped to maintain this environment in an original state, for the land cannot be easily used for farming or human settlement. Today, a large number of native species can still be found in the forests of this area.

The New Zealand pigeon is easy to spot among the thick treetops of the beeches. It has an olive green head and breast with copper reflections, a purplish brown back, a bright white underside, and a crimson beak.

The spotted flycatcher flutters in a constant hunt for insects, holding its large tail open like a fan. The black variation of this bird is rarely seen here, although dark colors are common in many species of New Zealand birds. Dark-colored birds are often found in dense, humid forests where bright colors would increase their chances of being seen by birds of prey. The tui, a greenish blue honeyeater that can mimic human speech, is common in these forests. The green acanthus, distinguished by its long, pointed beak and a short tail, lives among the branches of bushes. This native bird, barely 3 inches (7 cm) long, is the most common bird of the forest.

All these birds are preyed upon by the forest falcon, the only native bird of prey that is active during the day. The Morepork owl and the extremely rare smiling owl feed on rodents, small birds, and moths. These small, nocturnal birds of prey occupy ecological niches equivalent to those of the European owls.

Kea, Kaka, and Kakapo

New Zealand is inhabited by the kea, one of the most

unusual parrots of the world. This olive-green parrot is about the size of a crow and has rounded wings and a brilliant orange coloring on its underside. Its beak is long and curved. It lives only on the South Island, where it originally inhabited the plateaus of lower mountain regions swept by strong winds. The kea often entered the forests, where it found fruit, roots, honey, and other plant substances, as well as insects and larvae. During the winter, it migrated to the lower zones and sometimes to the coast.

The keas have become more widespread since the arrival of Europeans. This is surprising, since they have been extensively hunted. They were thought to be predators of sheep, although there is not proof that keas have ever killed sheep. Nevertheless, keas are not well liked by New Zealand ranchers.

Keas not only have to defend themselves from hunters,

The reproductive behavior of the kakapo is not unique. It is also found in other species of completely different families and orders. This behavior is based on stiff competition among the males, who show off to the females in special arenas called "leks." The arena is made up of a series of holes that are marked by branches and rocks *(diagram on the left)*. These holes are connected by "avenues" *(diagram on the right)*. The females watch from a distance, then move closer, and finally decide to accept the advances of a particular male. Often, just a few of the males are chosen by the females. The males mate with as many females as possible.

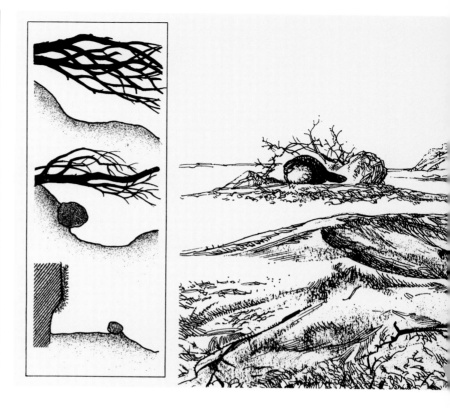

but they must also defend their nests from other predators. The most common of these are ermines and rats, which destroy their eggs and young. Despite their many enemies, the keas are still widespread and are not afraid of people.

The kaka birds populate the woods and forests of both islands of New Zealand. These birds are close relatives of the keas but are much more widespread. The kaka, however, is a brighter color than the kea. The upper part of its beak is also shorter than that of the keas. The kaka birds are generally protected and respected. However, in some areas they are mistaken for the keas and therefore hunted by sheep ranchers.

The kakapo parrot is one of the rarest and most interesting birds in the world. Unlike the other members of the parrot family, the kakapo has nocturnal habits. Other differences are its preference for living on the ground and its unique mating habits. Its feathers are not particularly showy. Their greenish and yellowish green colors are ideal for hiding in the forest. This parrot is about 25 inches (64 cm) long and is the heaviest-known parrot. The male can

weigh over 7 pounds (3 kg), and the female weighs an average of 3 pounds (1.6 kg). Like the owls and screech owls, it has long feathers located at the base of the beak. These long feathers cover the bird's neck, making its face appear rounded like the face of an owl. Although its wings are developed, the muscles that move them are very weak. As a consequence, the kakapo is unable to fly. When necessary, however, it can clear small obstacles by batting its wings very hard. It eats plants mainly but has been known to eat small lizards and insects, too.

These birds generally nest once every two to four years. This occurs from September to December, which is the spring and summer season in the Southern Hemisphere. The mating ritual of the kakapo deserves special attention because it is unique among the parrot family. During the mating season, every male prepares a "singing arena" by digging a series of holes in the ground. These holes measure from 1 to 2 feet (30 to 60 cm) in diameter and 2 to 8 inches (5 to 20 cm) in depth. Most often, the arena is built on a hill.

Every male maintains a variable distance from the

The black flycatcher is the rarest among the many insect-eating birds of New Zealand. Its extinction was prevented by the New Zealand Wildlife Service. Other similar species also exist in New Zealand.

arenas of its competitors. The arenas are complicated constructions, and the kakapo uses the same one year after year. From the singing arena, the male makes a low, booming sound. At the same time, it lowers its head and puffs up its thorax (part between neck and abdomen) until it looks like a giant ball. It also begins a kind of "dance," moving backward and slowly flapping its wings.

The females approach the arenas for short, unpredictable, and rare visits. Even after many hours of observation, researchers have not been able to witness the mating of the kakapos. They have only been able to trace the movements of the birds by their tracks. The female lays three or four eggs in a nest built in a tree cavity and sits on the nest to keep them warm. The female cares for the young when they hatch.

The kakapos were discovered and described for the first time just in the last century. However, they had been commonly found throughout New Zealand before then. Unfortunately, their numbers have been declining since the beginning of this century, partly because of the introduction of European animals such as cats, rats, and weasels to the area. These animals are predators of the kakapos. The decline of the kakapo population is also partly due to the changes in the forest habitat brought about by deer, which were also imported from Europe.

A Successful Rescue

The New Zealand Wildlife Service has been successful in preventing the extinction of the black flycatcher. This species, which was widespread in the past century, had become nearly extinct by 1860. This was due to the introduction of rats as well as the destruction of their tree habitat (deforestation). In 1973, only seventeen adult black flycatchers and one young remained in a small area on the island of Little Mangere. The New Zealand Organization for the Conservation of Animals began a program to save these birds. The organization planned to transfer them to nearby Mangere Island, where the habitat of the species was to be restored through the planting of at least a hundred thousand trees.

Unfortunately, after only three years, the already small population of black flycatchers was reduced to just two pairs and three unmated males. Therefore, it became necessary to take immediate action to save the species, without waiting for the growth of new trees. The two pairs of black

The Hawaiian seal is part of a small group of tropical seals of the monk seal subfamily. It is similar to both the Mediterranean monk seal and to the West Indies monk seal. Unfortunately, this animal has a population of only 700,500 today. Even fewer Mediterranean monk seals exist. The West Indian monk seal may already be extinct.

Two male deer stand guard on the banks of Lake Wakatipu on the South Island. The European deer found its ecological niche completely unoccupied in New Zealand. These herbivores spread everywhere because they had no predators. The damage caused to the environment by these animals is much greater in the long term than the economic benefits derived from their meat and antlers.

flycatchers were moved to an already existing wooded area on Mangere. The black flycatcher normally lays a second nest of eggs if the first is lost. Because of this characteristic, the conservation workers transferred the first eggs to the nests of other bird species that hatched them. This made it possible to double the number of young in every mating season. The result was a faster growth in the population of this species. The program was successful, and in 1983 it was even possible to move two pairs to another island.

Today this species numbers several dozen individuals

who live on the two islands. Though it is still in danger of extinction, the species has a good chance of surviving.

The European Colonization

The islands of New Zealand were completely untouched until about the year 1000, the approximate date of the first landing of Polynesians who came in search of new lands. Changes on the islands came about immediately, as the Polynesians began to hunt the native animals.

The first colonists hunted the giant moas. These animals were a source of clothing (feathers) and meat for the colonists. By the time of the second Maori migration, only a few moas were left. The Maori introduced the domestic dog and the rat. Other than two species of bats and a seal species that were native, the dog and rat were the only mammals on the islands.

But the greatest changes in the ecological balance of these lands came about when Captain Cook arrived. Following sailors' customs of the time, Cook's men planted cabbage, beets, and potatoes, which were to be used as food supplies for the coming voyages. Pigs, goats, and sheep were left to freely graze in order to have a future supply of meat. In this way, the English colonists introduced many animals and plants to the island. The colonists felt that bringing familiar animals to the islands would help create an environment similar to the homeland they had left.

Many of the colonists' animals were herbivores— animals that feed on grass and other plants. Herbivores introduced to the islands easily survived. This was possible because they did not have to compete with native herbivores for available space and food.

Many small predators were also introduced. These included ermines, weasels, and ferrets, as well as dogs and cats that had escaped into the wild. Although they preyed on native birds, these small predators had no effect on the increasing populations of imported herbivores. Because they had no predators, the populations of European deer, sambar, hare, rabbit, and other animals increased rapidly. They were so numerous that their eating habits destroyed much of the plant cover. In time, this caused a decrease in the populations of a number of native animal species that depended on the plant cover. Finally, many of them completely disappeared.

The importation of deer directly from Great Britain is a good example of what may occur if the population of a

Tropical vegetation is lush on the island of Oahu (Hawaii). This famous tropical paradise has not been protected from overdevelopment. The original forests of these islands have been reduced to a very small area. The disappearance of the forests has caused a great decline in the islands' animal populations. In the past 1,500 years, fifty of the eighty native bird species have become extinct. During the same time period, forty-five new species have adapted to the area.

particular herbivore is not controlled. Up until 1930, it was illegal to kill deer, and by that time the herds had begun to interfere with farming and ranching. Professional hunters were hired to reduce the number of these animals. In just twenty years (with a brief interruption during World War II), at least 2.4 million deer were killed. Hunters even shot the deer from helicopters, which allowed them to chase the deer in areas without passable roads. It was impossible to remove the bodies of the deer from these areas, and they were left to decay where they had been shot. At a certain point it became obvious that a large quantity of recoverable meat was being wasted. New Zealand thus began to export deer meat in addition to its already-famous lamb meat. When the export of venison was begun, the deer showed a decline in numbers for the first time since they had arrived in New Zealand. In fact, they were nearly in danger of becoming extinct. Although the naturalists wanted to restore the environment to its original state (without the European deer), the meat export business had become too important by then. The extinction of the deer in New Zealand was not acceptable for economic reasons, and since 1970, ranchers have obtained licenses from the government to raise the animals. The areas chosen for large, fenced ranches were originally not suitable for any other purposes. They now make up the richest pastures in New Zealand.

Venison is sold at a price that is about twice as high as the price of beef or lamb. The antlers of these deer are also in great demand in the Chinese and Korean markets. According to many Oriental people, the "velvet" that covers the new antlers has magical powers. They also believe the velvet can help restore sight and hearing and work as a medicine against certain diseases. Although there is no medical proof of these claims, the beliefs have created another business opportunity for deer ranchers. Some importers in China and Korea pay as much as one hundred dollars per pound for the "velvet," and an adult deer can supply up to nine pounds per year.

Obviously, in New Zealand the deer is no longer considered a simple pest. It has become an important economic resource. However, deer still destroy forest environments and thus threaten the survival of some of the most interesting species of New Zealand.

THE ARCHIPELAGOES

Many archipelagoes and little islands of various origins are scattered throughout the Pacific. The island groups closest to Australia are called "Melanesia." The main Melanesian archipelagoes are Bismarck, the Solomon Islands, New Hebrides, New Caledonia, and the two larger islands of Fiji. All of them have mountain ridges and lowlands covered with a tropical jungle. The names *Polynesia* and *Micronesia* refer to the volcanic and coralline island groups found toward the center of the Pacific Ocean.

Colonization and Native Life Forms

Not all the Polynesian archipelagoes were formed in the same way. Some islands have a volcanic origin, and others have a coralline origin. This is consistent with the theory that the atolls were formed on ocean volcanoes or on volcanic islands that later sank.

Although there are numerous island groups, they are separated by considerable distances. It is thus remarkable that plant and animal species have been able to spread from island to island and from faraway continents to these island groups. As a result of this spreading, the plant and animal communities on these islands are actually quite similar from a biogeographical viewpoint. (Biogeography deals with the distribution of animals on the earth.)

The main characteristic of the islands is the scarcity of animals. Only a few were able to reach the islands because of the great distances between them. Almost all of these animals are distantly related to Asiatic or Australian species, except for the American species that later colonized the islands.

The animals settled more quickly in the archipelagoes closest to the Australian coasts, and so these islands have many different groups. Only the species that were able to survive long voyages were able to colonize the most distant islands. Consequently, fewer animal species exist on the islands farthest to the east. Although there is less variety on the eastern islands, there are more native forms and unique species found there. The western Pacific islands are inhabited by 225 species of birds, of which 27 percent are native. In the eastern Pacific, there are only 42 species, and 78 percent of them are native.

The gray-headed blackbird is a good example of how native birds developed into a variety of forms because of their isolation. A different form of this bird species appears on every one of the islands of Fiji. On Ngau, the bird is

Opposite page: Caledonia on the eastern coast of the island near Hienghene offers fabulous scenery.

45

The iguana of the Fiji islands is a large lizard. The Fiji Islands mark the only place on earth where both the lizards of the iguana family and the agamid lizards live. The iguana is typically found in the Americas and Madagascar. The agamid lizards, on the other hand, are typically found in Europe, Africa, Asia, and Australia.

completely black, while on Taveuni, it is black with a gray head. On Kaydavu, it is black with a red head. This isolation of birds led not only to the evolution of unique species, but also to the evolution of unique genera. An example of this is the kagu of New Caledonia, which is the only species of its family on the islands.

Of all the vertebrates, the birds have had the greatest success in colonizing the islands of the Pacific because of their ability to fly. It is much harder for amphibians and reptiles to cover distances, so they are not found today on most of the islands. However, geckos and other lizards spread with the migration of Polynesian peoples. It is also difficult for mammals to cross the open sea, although there were migrations of a few marsupials, which are mammals that carry their young in a pouch. Among these migrating marsupials are Polynesian rats and certain bats. The fruit-eating bats and the insect-eating mouse-eared bats came to

Below: Most of the plants and animals that live in the Pacific archipelagoes today colonized the different islands by moving from west to east.

Following pages: A white tern takes food to its young. The areas of this species are particularly widespread in the Pacific Ocean, although it is found in all of the tropical seas of the world. Unlike its relatives that nest on the ground, the white tern lays just one egg that it balances in the branches of trees. This bird is unusually tame around humans.

the islands from Malaysia and New Guinea. The hairy-tailed bats on the Hawaiian Islands, however, came from America.

Some islands were once connected to larger land masses. Islands were formed when parts of land broke away from the continent. The animals left on these islands evolved differently from those on the continents, even though they kept many similarities to their relatives on nearby continents.

Animal colonization on volcanic or coralline islands is a different process. When these islands emerge, they have no life forms whatsoever. Even so, spores of fungus and ferns soon reach the new island, carried by air currents and typhoons. When fast air currents hit the peaks of volcanic islands, their water vapor condenses and turns to rain. The water vapor on the seeds and spores makes them heavy and causes them to fall to the ground. Here they may eventually sprout and take root. The wind also carries "air plankton," or tiny insects and spiders. Some insects and birds are carried far from their normal habitats by the wind and end up flying to new islands.

Seeds, spores, and even land animals can also be carried by objects floating on the water. Most fish that live near the coast and in surface waters cannot survive long journeys in the open sea. They are thus less likely to reach the new islands. Migratory birds, however, are very important in

the colonization of new islands. They carry seeds to the new islands in the mud caked on their claws, in their feathers, and in their digestive systems.

The settlement of plants and animals on a new island takes place in a definite order. Each new inhabitant improves the conditions for the others. For example, the lichens and fungi help prepare the soil for leafy plants. Insects can then feed on the plants. Birds and other vertebrates then feed on the insects.

This order of colonization was shown on the island of Krakatoa in 1883. In that year, a volcano destroyed all plant and animal life on the island. Just nine months after the volcano exploded, researchers found a spider on one of Krakatoa's islands. By 1908, the islands were inhabited by insects, lizards, snakes, land birds, and some mammals.

Changes on the Islands

The number of species of animals and plants on an ocean island is related to the island's distance from the continents, its size, and the variety of different habitats or environments on the island.

In 1963, American ecologists introduced the theory of "island biogeography." This theory states that the number of species of plants and animals found on an island is the result of migration and extinction. Factors that affect the number of species found on an island include the size of the island, its distance from the continent, relief, or differences in the elevation of land form, forest, and bodies of water.

All research carried out in the last ten years on island populations has been influenced by the original theory. Previously, zoologists often counted only the number of different species, not the population of each species. In other words, they never measured the density of the different populations. (Density refers to the number of individuals of a particular species in a given area.) Observing the density of a species is very important to understanding an island's biogeography. An island where a species exists but is rare is much different from another island where the same species is common. Each animal has a specific position in the ecology. It is both a predator and a food source for other predators. If the animal becomes rare, the animals it preys upon might increase in numbers. Those animals might then become a more important food source for another species.

Island biogeography is much more complicated than the theory suggests. Actually, recent research shows that

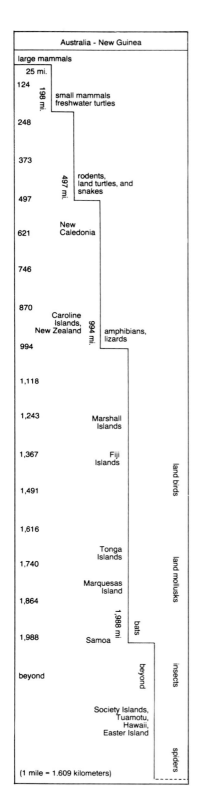

predation is a more important factor than the size of the islands and their distance from the continents. American researchers have recently studied the distribution of spiders on the smallest islands of the Bahamas. Although these islands are not in the Pacific, they can be used as an example for this theory. The researchers found that the spider populations were affected not only by their distance from the larger islands, but also by the presence or absence of the predatory lizard *Anolis sagrei*. Even on the closest, most easily reached islands, there were few spiders if this little reptile was present. The density of spiders greatly increased if the lizard had not yet reached the island.

The presence or absence of plant and animal species on an ocean island, as well as their population density, is influenced by many factors. Because of this, it is practically impossible for two different islands to have identical communities of plant and animal life. Every island is a world in itself, with its own characteristics, its own native forms, and its own natural balance. The balance can be upset at any time by the arrival of a new species. It can also be completely changed by the careless action of human beings.

New Caledonia

One of the largest islands of Melanesia and of the entire Pacific, New Caledonia is found about 60 miles (100 km) from the coast of Queensland (northern Australia). This island consists of 3,882 sq. miles (10,058 sq. km). A mountain ridge that reaches over 5,577 feet (1,700 m) crosses the island. Large rain forests are found in its lowest areas. Temperate forests of antarctic beech trees are found in its highest zones, and there are numerous large, flowering shrubs in these forests.

No mammals or amphibians are native to New Caledonia. However, the island has at least sixty-eight species of birds, some of which are truly surprising native forms. The strangest bird is the kagu, a rail-like bird that cannot fly. Because of the long tuft of feathers on its head, the kagu looks a bit like a stocky gray heron. It is quite large, growing to about 20 inches (50 cm).

The kagu lives in dense mountain forests. Because of the imported predators in these forests—especially dogs, rats, and pigs—it has become rare and is in danger of extinction. Fortunately, there are many kagus in zoos, and the species easily reproduces in captivity.

The kagu is not found in the wild anywhere outside of New Caledonia. In its native forests, which are slowly being cut down, the kagus feed on snails and worms. They lay only one egg and nest on the ground. When these birds are in danger, they spread their wings, revealing a display of white, black, and brown stripes that look like the colored stripes of the South American sun bittern. The origin of the South American sun bittern is still unknown, but it is almost certainly a relative of the kagu.

Another unique bird that exists only in New Caledonia is the horned parakeet, a beautiful green parrot about a foot (30 cm) long. It has a tuft similar to that of the cockatoo, although the horned parakeet's tuft is not erect. This bird is most often found throughout the reserve of the Blue River Forest.

The Fiji Islands

The Fiji archipelago is located halfway between New Caledonia and Polynesia. It includes 320 islands, of which

about 100 are inhabited. The entire territory covers 7,053 sq. miles (18,272 sq. km) mostly belonging to the two main islands, Viti Levu and Vanua Levu.

Some of these islands originated from volcanoes, while others are the remains of continental fragments. The Fiji Islands also include barrier reefs and atolls. The two largest islands are mountainous and covered by rain forests. Occasionally the rainfall in Fiji amounts to nearly 10 feet (3,000 mm) per year.

The fauna or native animals of these remote Pacific islands include two species of frogs and toads. Fiji is the farthest point these animals have reached in the Pacific. Four snakes and various lizards, including an agamid lizard and an iguana, also exist on the islands. The agamid lizard has a primitive form, while the iguana has a more modern form. Madagascar, a large island off the coast of Africa, is inhabited by modern iguanas but lacks the primitive agamid lizards. The presence of an iguana in the Pacific so far from the Americas is surprising.

There are sixty-seven species of birds on the islands. Three beautiful native species of fruit-eating doves, each one living in a different group of islands, are found in Fiji.

Birds of the Pacific islands include *(from left to right)*: a pair of horned parrots of New Caledonia, a blue lorikeet of Tahiti, a bird of the Diduncolo genus Samoa, and a pair of red parrots of the Fiji Islands.

The orange dove lives on Vanua Levu and Tavenuni, and the gold dove lives on Viti Levu. The yellow-headed dove lives on Kandavu and Ono. These colorful birds live in the tropical forests and eat fruit, berries, seeds, and insects.

Another special feature of Fiji is the beautiful shiny red parrot, an elegant bird about 18 inches (45 cm) long. Its back is green and blue, and its breast is red or brownish red. This bird is not found on the large islands, but several different varieties are found on other smaller islands.

Another beautiful native parrot is the collared lorikeet, which is found only on the large islands. It is smaller than the red parrot, but it has equally splendid colors. The colorful parrots eat fruit, berries, and seeds. The collared lorikeets prefer to eat the nectar of coconut palm flowers.

Samoa and Tonga

Less than a few hundred miles (several hundred km) to the east of Fiji are the Tonga Islands to the south and the Samoan Islands to the north. Tonga is a group of about 150 islands and islets situated about 20 degrees latitude south and between 173 and 176 degrees longitude west. Their total area is about 270 sq. miles (700 sq. km).

According to some botanists, coconut palms *(as seen here)* originated in Southeast Asia. Others believe they originated in South America. The species is widespread today along the coasts and islands of the Pacific and Indian oceans. The seeds of this tree can sprout even after they have been in salt water for a long time. The trunks are used for lumber. The native people of the islands use the leaves to make mats. They drink the juice of its fruit and eat the buds. The fibers of the wood are used to make rope, brushes, and baskets. The tree also produces coconut oil.

The Tonga Islands are located along two more or less parallel lines oriented in a northeast-southwest direction. They rest on two underwater ridges. The western ridge has a relatively gentle slope, while the eastern ridge descends steeply into the oceanic trench called the "Tonga Trench." At nearly 35,702 feet (10,882 m) below sea level, it is one of the deepest trenches on earth. The western ridge is made up of ten volcanic, mountainous islands covered with dense plant life. The eastern ridge is coralline.

The Samoan Islands lie a little to the north of Tonga. They are volcanic islands and are also composed of an eastern and a western group. The largest island is Savaii, which is 662 sq. miles (1,715 sq. km) in area. It is a huge volcanic cone whose highest peak, Mount Silisili, stands 6,050 feet (1,844 m) tall. There are about fifty smaller volcanic cones at various elevations.

The climate of Samoa is distinctly equatorial. The animal life here is not as dense as it is in Fiji, but it is more dense than the fauna of the Tonga Islands. There are about thirty species of birds in Samoa. The *Didunculus strigirostris* is one of the most interesting of the native birds. This bird resembles the now-extinct dodo bird of the island of Mauritius. It is similar to the dove but has a beak similar to that of a bird of prey. It has black-blue feathers with green reflections. Its wings and tail are brown, and it lives in the dense forests of the two largest islands—Savaii and Upolu. The bird finds most of its food on the ground. It feeds on berries, fruit, and other plant material. When sensing danger, it quickly flies into the trees. Besides an oversized beak, this bird has another oddity. It seems to be able to use its claws to hold its food. This behavior has not been observed in any other pigeon, but it is common among parrots.

French Polynesia

The archipelagoes of French Polynesia are found farther east, beyond the Tonga and Samoan Islands. French Polynesia includes the Society Islands, Marquesas Islands, Austral Islands (also called the Tubuai Islands), and the Tuamotu Archipelago.

The Society Islands, which include the famous island of Tahiti, are made up of fifteen volcanic islands. They are characterized by bold mountainous landscapes, difficult to reach valleys, picturesque gorges, and a narrow band of coral along their coasts where people live.

The sooty tern is the most "oceanic" of all the terns. It is widespread in the tropical zones of all the world's oceans. Often it flies with ships in high seas far away from the coast.

Tahiti is the most typical and important of these islands. It consists of two great volcanic cones that reach over 7,352 feet (2,241 m) in elevation. Streams flow from the summit of these volcanoes, carving out deep ravines and forming spectacular lakes and waterfalls. Almost all of the inhabitants of Tahiti live along the coast, even though there are inhabitable stretches of land that reach toward the mountainous interior. Beyond the narrow coastal strip, the landscape rises abruptly.

The vegetation, or plant life, is so dense that it is passable only if one uses a machete. It is necessary to use a guide to climb to the rough rapids of Vahiria Lake. This is the only volcanic lake of the entire South Pacific that is populated by huge black eels. The eels are more than 3 feet (1 m) long and as thick as a person's leg.

Another special feature of this island is the splendid lory of Tahiti, a nectar-eating parrot that has a light-blue back and a white underside. It originally existed on Tahiti, Moorea, Metia, Bora-Bora, Huahine, and Scilly. Today, it is no longer found on Tahiti, Moorea, or Bora-Bora. It has survived only on some little atolls of the Tuamotu Islands which, because of their size, cannot support large populations. This splendid bird may be in serious danger of becoming extinct.

There are not many birds on the Society Islands. Tropic birds, small white terns, small green pigeons, kingfishers, and others nest on Moorea. No mammals or native amphibians are found on the Society Islands, although there are some native reptiles in the form of small lizards.

The most scattered archipelago of Oceania is that of the Tuamotu Islands. This archipelago is made up of about seventy islands spread in a southeast-northwest direction over more than 1,243 miles (2,000 km), all the way from the Gambier Islands to north of the Society Islands. These coralline atolls are flat and low and most are small. The total area of the group is 353 sq. miles (915 sq. km). The coasts are generally fringed with coral reefs and characterized by white beaches formed by the build-up of sand and eroded coral. Coconut palms grow beyond the beach on a thin strip of land that forms the lagoon. The lagoon is seldom completely closed off from the sea.

Finally, the Marquesas Islands, located 808 miles (1,300 km) northeast of Tahiti, consist of eleven large, high, fertile islands. The highest peak is Mount Pout-tai-nui, on the island of Ua-Pau, which is over 4,429 feet (1,350 m) above sea level. The animal species here are even more scarce than they are on the Tonga Islands. There are only eleven species of land birds, five species of lizards, and no mammals or amphibians.

Pitcairn and Easter Islands

Pitcairn Island lies east of the Society Islands. It was settled by English sailors who mutinied against their commander on board the ship *Bounty*. The island is steep and heavily forested. Beyond Pitcairn is tiny, isolated Easter Island. It lies about 950 miles (1,500 km) from Pitcairn, and 2,287 miles (3,680 km) from South America. Easter Island is a volcanic island, famous for its monuments of giant human heads sculpted in stone.

Easter Island was not always as barren as it is today.

The castor-oil palm is a "milky" plant that originated in Asia and Africa. It was grown for its oil up until the time of the ancient Egyptians (four thousand years ago). Today, it exists in all the tropical zones of the world, including Easter Island where this photograph was taken.

Not long ago it was covered with dense plant life, which was later completely destroyed by humans. In 1983, two scientists found the remains of fruit from an ancient palm tree in a cave near Ana Okeke on Easter Island's Poike peninsula. The best-preserved remains of these plants were later examined by a group of British and Chilean researchers. They found that the fruits were from 780 to 860 years old. Because the remains of the fruits were not in good condition, the scientists were not able to determine their species. However, they were able to determine that the fruits came from a palm that is now extinct. The palm was probably very similar to the *Jubaea chilensis* palm, which still exists on the island.

Before 1983, fossils of palm pollen had been found on the island. Their exact species is still unknown, but the fossils prove that the island was covered with dense forests. The Moai people, who were the builders of the giant statues that are the symbols of Easter Island today, began cutting down the trees in about the year 1000.

Some of the local legends describe an ancient tree called the "makoi nau opata." According to the legends,

The spectacular crater of Rano Kau Volcano is found on Easter Island.

these bore edible fruit, so they may have actually been the trees whose fossils were found. If the extinct palm was similar to the existing palm, it would have had a straight, sturdy trunk. These trunks could have been made into levers used to move the giant statues. The trunks would also have been smooth enough to be used as rollers for moving heavy objects on the ground. The use of such instruments might explain how the huge statues were moved to their sites.

The construction of the giant Moai statues ended suddenly in 1680, perhaps just at the same time as the palm became extinct. A violent period of continual wars and cannibalism followed. This led to the extinction of the people on the island as well. By destroying the plant life of the island, the humans actually caused their own extinction.

Rats may also have been one of the causes of the trees' disappearance. The scientists found rodents' teeth marks on the ancient palm fruit remains. By eating the fruit of the palm, the rats prevented the seeds from sprouting. Thus, the species may have disappeared both because of humans who cut down the adult trees, and because of rodents who, by eating the seeds, prevented new trees from growing.

A sea fan is a beautiful example of the corals of the barrier reefs. In many atolls of the Pacific, underwater life is as rich and varied as life on land is scarce. The most isolated and remote islands are likely to have more native life forms.

Many Polynesian rats inhabited Easter Island when it was still covered with palms. They had probably come to the island with the first settlers. They later became extinct due to the competition with the European rat, which arrived on the island with the European settlers.

The Mariana, Caroline, and Marshall Islands

The westernmost region of the Pacific, north of the equator and New Guinea and east of the Philippines, is dotted with thousands of little islands, altogether known as Micronesia. Micronesia is made up of the Mariana, Caroline, and Marshall islands, which cover a total area of 531

sq. miles (1,375 sq. km). These archipelagoes extend toward South Asia. Micronesia and South Asia have similar types of plant and animal life.

The Mariana Islands are a chain of volcanic and coralline islands. They are made up of fourteen major islands and many little uninhabited islands, most of which are atolls. The animal life on the Marianas is relatively abundant. It includes various species of lizards and many species of birds that are now endangered species, due mostly to human activities.

Guam, a small island of the Mariana Islands, is a perfect example of an island whose birds face extinction because of humans. Tropical forests still cover most of this island, which is 212 sq. miles (549 sq. km) in area. Its bird life was studied at length by Mark Jenkins, an American ornithologist. He found thirteen species of forest birds on the island, and all but two of them were native. Jenkins' observations in 1978 and 1979 showed that most of the native birds that were common until the beginning of the 1960s began to decrease rapidly in number in a short time. Today, at least four species are in danger of extinction. The surviving populations of almost all the others are found only in a small area on the northern part of the island.

Normally, birds become extinct because of imported predators, storms, disease, or because their environment is destroyed. None of this is true of Guam. The imported predators, which include certain mammals and snakes, reached the island as far back as 1890. The decline of the birds, however, began eighty years later. Typhoons have not become more intense or frequent in the past few years, and vast primitive forest areas still exist.

However, pesticides, or insect poisons, were sprayed on the forests in large quantities. The first pesticides were sprayed by American soldiers trying to drive out the Japanese who were hiding there in World War II. Pesticides were later used by farmers. The insect-eating birds were most affected by the pesticides; tests carried out in 1975 showed that bird manure contained more pesticide substances than in previous years.

The planet is still not free from the danger of uncontrolled pesticide use. In the industrialized countries, there are now laws that control the use of pesticides. But in developing areas like Guam, the use of pesticides is practically unrestricted. Often in these countries, there are no environmental organizations or scientists who can prevent

the disasters that result from DDT and other pesticides.

The Caroline Archipelago begins east of the Mariana Islands, beyond the Mariana Trench, which descends to over 36,161 feet (11,022 m). It is made up of more than nine hundred little islands in a chain running from east to west for a distance of about 1,900 miles (3,000 km). Plant life is scarce on the smallest and lowest atolls but lush on the larger islands. The animal life includes some rodents, bats, snakes, and lizards.

The Marshall Islands are found farther east, about halfway between New Guinea and Hawaii and just a little north of the equator. The largest atoll in the world, Kwajelein, covers 888 sq. miles (2,300 sq. km). It is found in these coralline islands. Other atolls here, like Bikini and Eniwetok, were the scene of nuclear experiments carried out by the United States between 1946 and 1958.

Hawaii

The Hawaiian Islands are eight volcanic islands. They are located right in the middle of the Pacific, at a latitude of

Among the various species of tropical boobies, the masked or blue-faced booby is the most similar in plumage to the gannets of the temperate zones. The colonies of this bird can be found in all of the oceans of equatorial and tropical latitudes.

62

A beach is lined with coconut palms on the Samoan Islands.

20 to 22 degrees north. The islands vary in size from 45 to 4,020 sq. miles (117 and 10,414 sq. km). All together they total 6,413 sq. miles (16,615 sq. km). Almost all the islands were formed by the overlayering of successive lava flows. Some of the volcanoes are very recent, while others are older and have already eroded. Some of these have been reduced to reefs covered with corals.

The largest island, Hawaii, is currently the only island with any real volcanic activity. The mighty peaks of Mauna Kea at 13,796 feet (4,205 m) and Mauna Loa at 13,677 feet (4,169 m) rise at the center of this island. Despite its slightly lower elevation, Mauna Loa is actually the larger. The base of this volcano rests on the ocean bottom at a depth of about 19,685 feet (6,000 m). At least 90 percent of all the solidified lava of Mauna Loa is below sea level.

The Hawaiian Islands extend like an arc from southeast to northwest. Beyond the islands of Kauai and Niihau, which are located at the northwestern tip of the arc, lies a series of low coralline islands. These white, dry islands cover fewer than a few thousand square miles. They include some small islands, such as Laysan, Midway, and Kure, which are famous for their colonies of marine birds.

Even though it is located at the level of the Tropic of

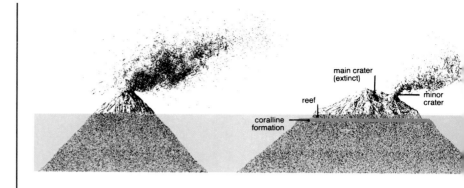

Above: A diagram follows the formation of a coralline atoll. At the far left, a new volcano emerges from the sea. The steep slopes of its cone form an island. Next, the main crater becomes extinct and almost disappears. A smaller crater opens, and the first corals begin to establish colonies in the shallow waters at the edge of the volcanic island. The volcanic island then sinks. The secondary crater then becomes inactive, and the coral reef continues to grow around it. In the last diagram on the right, the volcanic island has sunk completely, and the coral reef has grown around it. A lagoon is all that is left in the interior. *Below:* Mauna Kea is a volcano in the Hawaiian Islands.

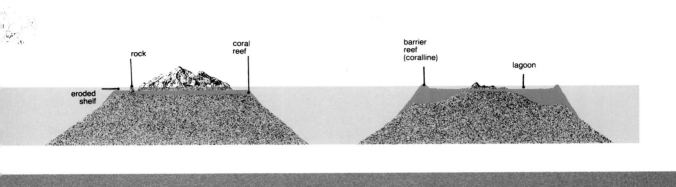

rock

coral reef

barrier reef (coralline)

lagoon

eroded shelf

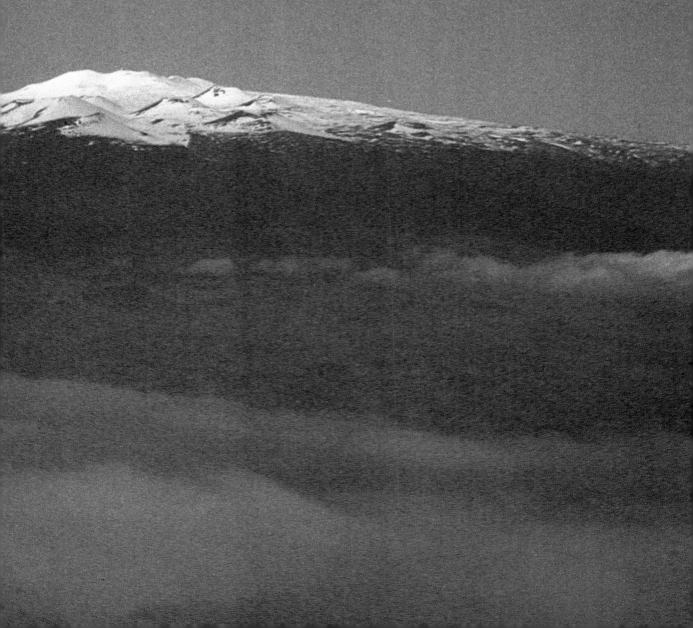

Cancer, where one would expect hot climates, the entire archipelago is characterized by mild, constant temperatures. In Honolulu, the average temperature in the hottest months, August and September, is 77°F (25°C). In the coldest months, January and February, the average temperature is 70°F (21°C). Rainfall varies greatly from area to area. Some parts in the mountainous areas of Kauai Island have an average annual rainfall of 460 inches (1,170 cm).

The smallest, lowest islands and the coastal plains of the larger islands may receive as little as 4 to 20 inches (10 to 50 cm) per year. In other areas, depending on the elevation, exposure, and other factors, there are moderate conditions that result in an extraordinary variety of plants and animals.

The first zone of plant life on the islands consists of a band of spiny bushes and various grasses on the coastal plains. Higher up is a thin forest cover of screw pines, hibiscus, and milo. The great koa acacias appear between 1,000 and 2,000 feet (300 and 600 m) above sea level. Sandalwoods also existed in this band at one time, but they have disappeared. Their extinction was caused by extensive cutting by the local population.

The ohias, ferns, and koas appear at higher elevations. Ferns make up an important part of the Hawaiian flora. There are about seventy species of ferns on the different islands. They have various sizes, ranging from the filmy fern, which is less than an inch tall, to the tree ferns that are 50 feet (15 m) and taller.

The Unusual Honeycreepers

Hawaii offers a great variety of ecological niches for animals. Some of the animals in these isolated environments have evolved into unique species. The birds are the most numerous of the vertebrate animals. There are about sixty native species on the islands as well as an incredible number of nonnative birds introduced by European and American settlers. The most interesting are the ones known as the honeycreepers.

The honeycreepers are a family of small perching birds that are completely different from any other birds on the islands. They developed in much the same way as the chaffinches that Charles Darwin studied on the Galapagos Islands. The honeycreepers probably originated from a small group of sparrows or honeycreeper warblers that came from the coasts of the Americas. After crossing more than 1,850 miles (3,000 km) of ocean, perhaps pushed along

Opposite page: The koa acacia tree grows from 1,000 to 3,000 feet (305 to 914 m) above sea level in Hawaii. The Hawaiian flora, like its fauna, includes many native species that do not exist in any other part of the world. Unfortunately, this wealth of life forms is in decline because of the environmental damage caused by humans over the centuries.

66

by a storm, the American birds found their perfect environment. The islands offered plenty of food, there was little competition for it, and there were few predators.

A fast evolutionary process then began. This resulted in the development of nine genera and twenty-seven species. Some of the species fed on nectar, some on insects, and others on seeds and fruit. The diet of the honeycreepers was similar to that of the chaffinches, finches, black-cap sparrows, and other nectar-eating sparrows. Since these latter birds did not exist on the islands, the Hawaiian honeycreepers were able to occupy the available environments without competing for food. The most common honeycreepers in the mountain forests are the insect-eating amakihi and the nectar-eating apapane and red honeycreepers.

A Dramatic Change in the Bird Population

The honeycreepers were not the only victims of the invading colonization of Hawaii by humans and the numerous animals they brought with them. Two American

The famous nene goose is the last of eight species of native Hawaiian geese. Seven native species of Hawaiian geese are now extinct because of human activities. The nene goose was saved by a conservation program begun in the 1950s.

paleontologists recently discovered that at least eighty native bird species existed on Hawaii before the Polynesian colonization of the island, which took place about a thousand years ago. Only forty-one of these native species still existed by 1778, when James Cook landed on the Hawaiian Islands. Later, the European colonization caused the extinction of more species. Today, only twenty-nine species exist on the islands.

The birds that disappeared before 1778 included at least seven species of geese. Many of them were unable to fly. The famous nene goose is the only surviving species. The original population of 25,000 nene geese decreased to just fifty before a program to breed them in captivity was begun in the 1950s. The program was successful, and the nene goose was saved from extinction. Other bird species that disappeared before 1778 include two ibises, seven flightless species of the rail family, a sea eagle, one sparrow hawk, three owls, two kinds of crows, one honeyeater, and at least fifteen species of honeycreepers. Originally there were at least forty-two species of honeycreepers. The most important causes of this dramatic change in the bird population were the cutting down of trees and the introduction of predators and competitors.

The Hawaiian Islands have experienced the largest

introduction of nonnative birds of any area on earth. In a recent book on this subject, the Australian ornithologist John Long lists about seventy species of birds that are new to the islands. Of these, forty-five have completely adapted to their new environment. Another twenty-five are still in the process of adapting and will probably survive. In comparison, New Zealand has only forty introduced species, North America has fifty-six, Australia has forty-four, and Europe has thirty-eight.

Some of the birds introduced into Hawaii are the Indian myna birds, the Japanese nightingale, white-eye birds, European skylarks, Shama blackbirds, and thrush-magpies of tropical Asia. Others include North American mockingbirds, various species of parrots, the Australian crested and striped dove, the common pheasant, and various species of francolins.

The environmental changes caused by so many new kinds of birds were not always good for the balance of nature on the islands. The enormous number of new species greatly changed the lives of the native species. Originally, as on many other oceanic islands, the few species present in the forests of Hawaii occupied rather large niches. Now, however, the competition for food has increased. Australian ornithologist Allen Keast found that out of the four most common species of birds in the forests of Kauai, only one was native. This bird is the red apapane. The other three originated in Asia.

Besides the apapane, there are still some native species that are common. For example, the amakihi, a honey-creeper, and the elepaio, a flycatcher, still exist. The Hawaiian goose or nene goose has returned to the dark lava beds that are its natural habitat. Another native species, the Hawaiian duck, whose population has also decreased, populates the wetlands of several national parks. Besides this rare duck, many native birds like the Italian cavalier and moorhens are found in the few remaining swampy zones. At sundown, the native short-eared owl patrols the area in search of rodents, its favorite food. This bird is widespread throughout the Southern Hemisphere, and it is thought to have been brought to Hawaii by strong winds.

As in all the other archipelagoes of the tropical Pacific, the small volcanic islands of Hawaii are home to thousands of marine birds. Countless flocks of birds like the sooty tern, the fool tern, and the more rare white fool tern gather on Moku Manu, the volcanic rocks near the island of Oahu. These birds gather every year for the mating season.

71

VERTEBRATE ANIMALS RETURNED TO THE SEA

Some of the vertebrate animals that lived in the sea evolved into amphibians that colonized the land. At a later time, however, some of them evolved into forms that returned to the aquatic environment. Many species of reptiles, birds, and mammals now spend their entire lives in or near the water. Some of their most important organs have adapted to their life there. As a result, life on land is now more difficult for them.

During the age when the reptiles were most numerous, the sea environment was populated by *ichthyosaurs*. These animals were similar to today's dolphins. They were excellent swimmers. The sea was populated by *tylosaurs* and *elasmosaurs*, which grew to almost 50 feet (15 m) long. These huge animals were characterized by long, snakelike necks.

Sea Turtles

Sea turtles have retained features that are common to those of land turtles. The structure of the sea turtles' shell has not changed. It has simply become flatter and lighter in weight, which helps them in swimming. Their strong legs have become flattened and function as "flippers." This feature, along with a flap of skin on the toes, makes swimming easy for them.

Today, five different species of turtles live in the seas. The loggerhead turtle, the hawksbill turtle, the green turtle, and the olive turtle belong to the sea turtle family. The leatherback turtle is in a family of its own.

The difference between the two families lies in the structure of the shell. Unlike other turtles, the leatherback turtle's shell is not covered with horned, rigid plates. Instead, it is covered with bonelike plates that are joined together and covered by tough, leathery skin.

All these species live in tropical or subtropical waters of both the Atlantic and the Pacific oceans. The leatherback turtle is the only one of the five species that does not have both an Atlantic and a Pacific species.

The green turtle lives in shallow waters of the open sea. These areas have rocky bottoms and are rich with plants. The green turtle feeds mostly on plants, preferring eel grass and turtle grass. This turtle was once common, but its numbers are rapidly decreasing due to hunting. The green turtle is hunted for its flesh and eggs. In certain areas, it is considered a delicacy.

The loggerhead turtle, which is smaller than the green

Opposite page: The loggerhead turtle is found in all three large oceans of the earth and even in many closed seas of the tropical and subtropical zones. They feed mostly on fish and jellyfish. They also eat crabs, sea urchins, and mollusks.

loggerhead turtle

common tortoise

Here, the loggerhead turtle is compared to a common tortoise from above and from the side. The common tortoise is a land animal, and the loggerhead is a sea turtle. The front legs of the tortoise have adapted to their digging function. Those of the sea turtle are shaped like fins and are used for swimming. The shell of the sea turtle is flat and has a more aerodynamic form. This also makes swimming easier. The land turtle's shell is more rounded and massive.

turtle, lives in bays along the coast. Occasionally it inhabits the areas where rivers meet the sea but is rarely found in the open sea. This turtle prefers to feed on animals.

The hawksbill turtle lives in deep waters with flat bottoms and few plants. Even though it is omnivorous, which means it eats both plants and animals, it prefers to feed on animals. This species' shell is covered with colorful, transparent scales. This makes the hawkbill turtle especially valuable as a material for jewelry, especially in Sri Lanka, Indonesia, and Japan.

The smallest marine turtles are the olive turtles, which are no more than 24 to 28 inches (60 to 70 cm) in length. They prefer deep waters and rarely come to the surface. Their diet is made up mostly of plants.

In spite of its great size, the leatherback turtle is certainly the best adapted to water life of all marine and land turtles. An adult of this species can be 8 feet (2.5 m) long and weigh between 1,500 to 1,800 pounds (700 to 800 kg). The leatherback turtle's enormous front flippers are so powerful that they can propel it nearly 330 feet (100 m) in just ten seconds. This is as fast as some of the best runners in the hundred-meter track event.

The green turtle, which is found in all the earth's oceans, is larger than the loggerhead. The adult green turtles eat mostly algae, while the young are carnivores. This species is heavily hunted for its flesh and eggs. Both are considered delicacies.

The leatherback turtle spends its life in the open waters far from the coast, where its enemies are sharks. It is an omnivore and feeds primarily on jellyfish, including the poisonous ones. This food preference causes survival problems for the leatherback turtle. Often the animal mistakes plastic bags, which now litter all the waters of the earth, for jellyfish. If a turtle eats a plastic bag, the bag can block its intestines and cause its death.

All sea turtles spend their lives under the water. This makes accurate and complete studies of them difficult, and little is known about their habits and behavior. They lead a more or less solitary life. The only time they are in groups is during the mating season, which takes place in the shallow waters near the coast, and they can be observed only when they come to the shore to lay their eggs. Sometimes the turtles migrate over long distances to reach the shore.

During the reproductive season, the females gather together in a large group to lay their eggs. For unknown reasons, they always land on the same beaches. It is possible that the females remember the beaches or that they are led by a natural instinct. Or perhaps the turtles get a sense of

A group of newly-hatched green turtles quickly crosses a short strip of beach to reach the safety of the sea. Predators manage to kill many of them before they do. Sometimes there are very few, if any, survivors. The species is threatened with extinction. This is not so much due to its traditional predators as it is to human activity. By building on the coastal environment, people destroy the turtles' nesting areas.

direction from the position of the sun and stars, or from their sense of smell or hearing.

The turtles are as awkward on land as they are agile in water. They almost seem to drag across the land when they come to lay their eggs. After having walked past the high tide limit, the female turtles dig deep holes and immediately begin to lay many eggs in them. The eggs are about the size of Ping-Pong balls and have a thick, flexible shell. After laying the eggs, the female covers the hole and smooths out the surface so that the nest is hidden. Then she goes back to the sea. Warmed from the sun's heat, the eggs incubate for about two months.

The female comes ashore seven or eight times in one reproductive season. She goes to a different beach each time and always lays the same number of eggs. This behavior assures the sea turtle of at least some offspring each season. This is especially important since a female turtle does not lay eggs every year, but rather every few years. The loss of an entire brood to a predatory animal or temperature extremes would decrease the species' chance of survival.

The eggs all hatch together at the end of the incubation period, and the young turtles climb out of the holes. This is one of the most critical moments of their lives. They have difficulty crawling across the sand to the water, which offers their only hope for survival. Very few are able to reach the water. Many of them are killed immediately by mammals and birds; and, once they reach water, sharks and other hungry fish prey on them. The low survival rate of young turtles is all part of nature's balance. Unfortunately, their survival is made even more difficult because of the extensive hunting by humans.

Sea Snakes

It is probable that some species of reptiles returned to the sea to take advantage of the abundance of food there. This is true of other vertebrate animals as well. Certain species of snakes developed important adaptations to a life in the sea. Even though sea snakes look like land snakes, their anatomy and body functions are remarkably different.

There are fifty species of sea snakes living in the tropical waters of the Pacific and Indian oceans. Their heads, necks, and upper parts are small compared to their abdomens. This enables them to cut through the waves more easily. The tail, which is very wide, functions like an oar. Their nostrils, like those of all animals that have returned to the water, are positioned on the upper part of the snout. A special structure keeps them sealed when they are underwater.

There are two subfamilies within the family of sea snakes, and each has different adaptations. The sea snakes of the Laticaudinae subfamily have overlapping scales on the back and large plates on the underside. The sea snakes of the Hydrophiidae subfamily have more specialized evolutionary adaptations than those of the Laticaudinae subfamily. Land snakes move by using the large scales of the belly. But the belly scales of the snakes of the Laticaudinae are almost as small as their back scales. The diameter of this

Above: A sea snake swims among the rocks.

Opposite page, from top to bottom: Shown are the position of the salt glands in a marine bird's skull (A); head of a booby with its nostril-less beak (B); a cormorant drying its nonwaterproof feathers in the sun (C); a white tern sitting on its egg, balanced on the branches of a palm (D).

snake's belly is four or five times greater than the diameter of its neck.

Unlike the turtles, sea snakes have no need to leave the water to reproduce. They do not lay eggs. Their young are born directly in the water, like the young of dolphins and whales.

All sea snakes are poisonous, and their poison is generally more dangerous than that of land snakes. The strength of their poison varies according to the marine environments in which they live. A more powerful poison is necessary in areas with rough waters, reefs, and lots of vegetation. This ensures that the prey quickly dies before it can get out of the snake's sight. A slower-acting poison would enable the prey to hide before dying.

Despite their ability to travel great distances, sea snakes generally prefer shallow waters rich with fish. The only species that prefers the open sea is the black-and-yellow sea snake, which has an odd hunting technique. By remaining motionless on the water's surface, it resembles a piece of floating wood. Little fish approach it out of curios-

ity, only to discover too late that the floating object is a deadly snake.

Marine Birds

Many species of birds have chosen the open sea as their habitat. They rely on the ocean for their food and fly to the land only to mate and lay eggs. These birds can be divided into two subgroups that have common features. One group consists of types that have adapted to life in the shallow waters of the continental shelf. The other group has adapted to the open sea.

In order to survive, these birds had to evolve a system that would enable them to eliminate excess salt. This is important, since their only water source is the salt water of the sea. Unlike the salt elimination process used by all land vertebrates, these birds developed special nasal glands. The glands are positioned on top of the head in special skull cavities. They work in much the same way as the kidneys. Their secretions enable the birds to get rid of the salt their bodies do not use.

The birds of the open sea also had to adapt to long-distance flight, which requires a lot of energy. Migratory land birds can fly only by flapping their wings. This type of flight, called "active flight," however, would certainly require too much energy for marine species. Therefore, they use a gliding type of flight, made possible by the special structure of their long, pointed wings. The gliders take advantage of the upward push of the wind as it blows across the waves. This push counterbalances the force of gravity. The bird "floats" on air and actually uses no energy except to keep its breast muscles tight enough to slightly move its tail feathers and wings.

Since they get their food from the water, these birds must also be excellent swimmers, which they are because of their webbed feet. The wings have not evolved into swimming organs because they are necessary for long-distance flight.

Marine birds use many different hunting techniques. Some, such as sea gulls, petrels, and forked-tail petrels, move along the water's surface by moving the tail and short wings. Others, like the boobies, tropic birds, and terns, hunt beneath the surface, though at different depths, diving from the air to catch fish. The albatross swims along the surface catching fish with its strong, hooked beak, while the pelicans dive almost like scuba divers. Only the diving petrel, a

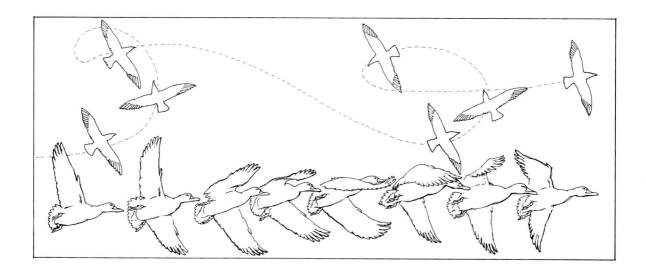

bird of the open sea, uses its wings for both flying and swimming. As a result of this special evolution, however, the diving petrel cannot glide.

Another adaptation to the water environment is the waterproofing of feathers. The birds continually smear their feathers with an oily secretion of a tail gland. The secretion causes the water to slide off without getting the under feathers wet.

These birds are found on land only during the nesting season, on rocky shores, or in the grassy areas of the coast. The nesting areas of continental shelf birds are close to an abundant food supply. These birds produce many offspring. The birds of the open sea, on the other hand, have to carry food over long distances to feed their young. They do not nest every year, but rather every two or three years.

Birds of the Continental Shelf

Birds of the continental shelf include boobies, tropic birds, frigate birds, and cormorants. The cormorants do not frequent the open sea as often as the others. Instead, they can often be observed standing perfectly still on rugged, rocky cliffs of the coast and nearby islands. They take to the air off the sides of the cliffs, their strong wings keeping them above the water's surface. The cormorants catch fish with their curved beaks, actually chasing fish by using their webbed feet to propel themselves under the water.

Cormorants are medium-sized birds averaging between 20 and 40 inches (50 to 100 cm) in length. They have long,

This diagram compares gliding flight to active flight. The gliding birds stay aloft with the help of sea breezes. They use the push supplied by the wind's upward motion. This push counterbalances the opposite force of gravity. There is no muscular energy wasted in gliding. A minimum amount of energy is used to keep the breast muscles taut and to gently adjust the position of the tail and feathers. Muscular energy is used by birds that fly by flapping their wings *(bottom of diagram)*.

The New Zealand sea gull is found in Australia, Tasmania, and South Africa as well as in New Zealand. It is smaller than the common European sea gull. The adults have white feathers and silvery-gray wings and backs. The tips of the white-spotted wings are black. These gulls have red feet and beaks.

thin necks, short, strong wings, and sturdy tails. The most widespread species on the islands and coasts of the Pacific Ocean is the common diving cormorant. This bird has shiny black feathers, and the underside of its "chin" and the sides of its head are white. Two white spots appear on the feathers of its legs during the mating season. This species lives in groups.

Unlike other marine birds, the cormorant's feathers are not waterproof. This is because the cormorants do not have a waterproofing gland. This lack may be an adaptation that enables these birds to catch fish beneath the water's surface. The birds are heavier when their feathers get wet. The added weight of the water in their feathers makes diving easier for them. But this weight is a disadvantage when the bird takes flight. To compensate for the added weight, the

Below: Fishing techniques of different species of cormorants are seen. *From top to bottom:* The guanay falls straight down into schools of fish at the water's surface and tries to grab them on impact. The common cormorant never simply falls. Instead, it dives into the water, swimming beneath the surface with its webbed feet. The wingless cormorant of the Galapagos Islands is unable to fly. It hunts fish along the shore. *Right:* The spotted cormorant is a species exclusive to New Zealand and Chatham Island.

cormorant actually uses the movement of its feet in the water as it takes off.

The cormorants nest in rocky environments. Their nests are made of algae and other marine plants stuck together with mud and fish remains. The female generally lays three eggs that are incubated for about four weeks. Young cormorants mature slowly. They leave their nests about fifty days after they have hatched. They become completely independent at about twelve weeks of age, but they do not grow their adult feathers and cannot mate until their third year of life.

These birds have a tremendous economic importance for human beings. Fishers around the world know that the presence of cormorants indicates the presence of fish. Although fishermen now use other methods to find fish, cormorant manure is still used as an organic fertilizer due to its high content of phosphates (salt of phosphoric acid). Cormorant manure was used as a fertilizer by the ancient inhabitants of Peru, a country with a huge cormorant population.

Cormorant manure is also part of the biological cycle of phosphorous, a nonmetallic chemical element. The manure is washed from the shore back to the sea. Its phosphates promote the growth of phytoplankton (microscopic plant organisms) in the ocean. The increased growth of plankton increases the production of zooplankton (microscopic animal organisms). This zooplankton is eaten by anchovies. Cormorants and other marine birds then eat the anchovies. Thus, cormorant manure is important for recycling phosphates back into the ocean waters.

Frigate Birds and Tropic Birds

The slender frigate bird, one of the most spectacular marine birds, is often seen in the skies over the tropical waters of the Pacific Ocean. The frigate bird is an excellent glider because of its long, thin, pointed wings, forked tail, and short legs. It often glides perfectly motionless in the air, ready to steal the fish that have been caught by other birds. The frigate birds, in fact, have adopted a piratelike hunting technique, and the boobies are most often their victims. The frigate birds chase and attack the boobies, forcing them to regurgitate their recently-caught prey. They will actually steal the fish away from the boobies in midair. The frigate birds also skim the water's surface to catch fish, the young of other birds, and sea turtles.

During courtship, the magnificent frigate bird puffs up his throat sack until it reaches an extraordinary size. In other seasons, the deflated sack hangs from the neck and breast of the bird.

84

The dark feathers of the male frigate bird become very colorful during the mating season. In addition, a large featherless area on its throat turns bright red. The throat also puffs up during courtship, a signal of sexual attraction to the females. At the same time, it is a warning signal to competing males.

The female lays only one egg in a nest it has built at the top of a shrub. The male and female take turns sitting on the nest to keep the egg warm, and the chick hatches after about fifty days. It depends on its parents for food for about four or five months.

Three types of frigate birds are widespread on the islands of the Pacific Ocean. These are the magnificent frigate bird, which is the most widespread; the ariel frigate bird, and the small frigate bird. All generally live in small groups.

The tropic birds are other birds of the pelican order. At first glance, these birds resemble sea gulls or other sea swallows. They can be distinguished by their tapered shape and their two tail feathers, which can be up to 2 feet (60 cm) long. There are three species: the white-tailed, the yellow-beaked, and the red-beaked tropic birds. The tropic birds can fly very fast and, like the sea swallows, they dive straight down into the water to catch fish.

The nesting areas of the tropic birds are generally scattered throughout hard-to-reach areas on the small Polynesian islands. Unlike pelicans and cormorants, young

86

A red-tailed tropic bird sits on its nest. This bird is widespread in the warmest regions of the Indian and Pacific oceans. Its normal plumage is tinted pink, and it has black spots above the eyes, on the joints of the wings, and on the sides. The long tail feathers make its total length an average of 3 feet (1 m).

A colony of Australian boobies is seen at Kidnappers Cape in New Zealand. The booby family includes species that inhabit both temperate zones and tropical zones. Both types are closely related and nest in colonies on small ocean islands. The northern boobies, the Cape boobies, and the Australian boobies are common in temperate zones.

tropic birds are covered with down, like sea gulls. When the eggs hatch, both parents leave the nest to search for food.

The young tropic birds are left to fend for themselves during this search. This is the most critical moment of their survival, for they are often attacked by adult birds of their own or other species. They develop a layer of fat within about ten or twelve weeks, which allows them to leave the nest and survive on the open sea.

Boobies

One of the most spectacular birds of the pelican order is the booby, a large bird whose wings and tail are bordered

in black. Several different kinds of boobies can be found in the Pacific. Some have light-blue feet, while others have red feet. The plumage of some species is completely dark. These birds have developed special physical characteristics with which they have adapted to life in the open sea. In fact, they land on the shore only for nesting.

The boobies are known for their remarkable dives. These birds can dive straight down for 100 to 160 feet (30 to 50 m) to catch fish. They minimize their impact with the water by closing their wings as they dive. Air sacks located just under the skin increase their ability to float. Out of the water, they breathe through the nostrils of the beak. While under the water, these nostrils are sealed to prevent water from entering. Boobies generally fish in schools of anchovies or sardines. Other marine birds learn of the presence of fish by sighting boobies diving into the water.

Boobies build nests with algae and grasses on the beaches of small, solitary islands. The female lays only one egg. Newly-hatched boobies are featherless and stay in the nest for two months. The adult feathers appear only in their fifth or sixth year.

Birds of the Open Sea

Four closely related families of the order of tube-nosed swimmer birds inhabit the open sea. These are albatrosses, shearwaters, stormy petrels, and diving petrels. All of them probably originated in the Southern Hemisphere. Some species have gradually colonized the North Pacific, North Atlantic, Indian Ocean, and Mediterranean, but the largest number of species is found in the Southern Hemisphere. The petrels are well adapted to the stormy southern seas where the winds are strong. In fact, they are so well adapted to the winds that they have trouble flying in the calmer equatorial areas.

The adaptations of these birds are even more remarkable than those of other marine birds. They have very long, slender, and flat wings that enable them to fly for long periods of time with minimum effort. They have webbed feet that are used as "brakes" when they land and as "propellers" when they swim. Their beaks are strong and curved. The upper beak has two nasal tubes that lead to openings on the top of the beak. The nasal tubes are connected to nerve networks associated with the sense of smell.

The birds locate food, nesting areas, and colonies of their own species with their sense of smell. All birds of this

order give off a strong, musky odor, which attracts each bird to colonies of its own species. The intense odor comes from an oily substance that is produced by stomach cells, where it is stored in great quantities. The oil has several functions. First, it is used to prevent the fermentation of food carried by adult birds to their young. Second, the birds use the oil to defend themselves against attacks by spitting it on their attackers. Finally, the stomach oil is added to the secretion of the oil gland to make their thick feathers even more waterproof.

Petrels, unlike other marine birds, are active at night, when their search for food is easier. Their diet consists of small fish, octopuses, squid, and shrimp. Like plankton, these animals live in deep water during the day and move to the surface at night.

Birds of the open sea mature slowly. They nest only once every two or three years, and their reproductive cycle is very slow, the formation of one egg taking a long time. The embryo also develops very slowly, as does the chick after hatching. The egg of the storm birds, the smallest species, incubates for forty days. The egg of the albatross, the largest species, incubates for eighty days. The smallest species care

Different marine birds have different feeding habits. *From left to right:* A frigate bird, recognized for its dark feathers and forked tail, chases a booby with the intention of stealing its fish. Next, a tern fishes in surface waters. To the right, a tropic bird (recognized by its long central tail feathers) and a booby dive straight down to catch fish at depths up to several yards.

Below: The black-browed albatross of New Zealand and the Southern Hemisphere is one of the world's largest marine birds. It nests on the small islands near Cape Horn, in the Falklands, Georgia, and the Kerguelen, Heard, Campbell, Antipodes, and Macquarie islands.

Following pages: The screaming albatrosses perform their mating "dance."

for their young for at least two months. Some albatrosses care for their young for nine to twelve months.

The young birds eat food that has been regurgitated by their parents. The food consists of a mixture of partially digested fish and stomach oil. This diet allows the young to build up a large amount of fat, which protects them from bad weather and helps them survive long periods with no food. It also enables them to survive even if their parents abandon them before they become independent.

During the mating season, the screeching of petrels and albatrosses can be heard throughout the atolls of the South Pacific. At least seven species nest in this part of the world. Two others, the Laysan albatross and the black-footed albatross, nest north of the equator on the Hawaiian Islands. More specifically, they nest on the Midway and Kure atolls, which are national animal refuges. There are many Laysan albatrosses. About 3 million of them exist in an area of just 12 sq. miles (31 sq. km).

The fascinating mating ritual of the albatrosses occurs in the month of October. The Laysan albatrosses, like all albatrosses, are monogamous, which means that they have

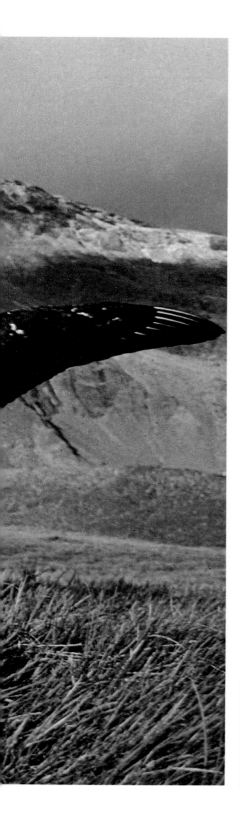

only one mate. The pair is actually mated for decades until one of the pair dies. This is true even though they sometimes spend only a few days together every year.

The mating season is long and involves a joint effort between the male and female. The female lays only one egg, and the male and female take turns keeping it warm. The male begins by sitting on the nest for at least three weeks. During this time the male does not eat or drink, and it loses up to 25 percent of its body weight. The female, meanwhile, soars above the sea in search of food. The female may travel up to a few thousand miles away to find it. A "biological clock" tells the female exactly when it is time to go back and take her turn sitting on the egg.

The male and female then take shorter turns keeping the egg warm. The egg hatches after a total of sixty to eighty days, depending on the species. The parents then go back and forth from land to sea for five to seven months. This assures the young of a meal about every two days. The two parents meet at the nest purely by accident during this period. When the young albatross is finally able to fly, each parent goes off by itself until the next mating season begins. At that time, they meet again in the same place. This is an extraordinary mating bond that involves complete fidelity and enormous common responsibilities. However, the pair is actually together for a total of just two or three days per year.

The mating dance is very important in beginning the relationship between the male and the female. It is possible that the mating dance serves to establish compatibility in view of the cooperative efforts required during nesting. It takes a long time for the young to learn the ritual, beginning in their third or fourth year of life on the island where they were hatched. The males finally become experts when they are seven or eight years old. At that time, they search for a mate in a new territory, attracting the attention of the unmated females by wailing. When a female responds to the male's call by kneeling, the dance begins. The male, standing straight and puffing up its breast, holds its head high and makes a low moan. The male then shakes itself, makes a different sound, and pecks its thigh while raising its wing. The female bobs its head. The dance continues with a variety of motions, screeches, and moans for about a quarter of an hour. After this dance, the two birds stand rigid, apparently uncertain of what to do. This dance is repeated until the two are "engaged." At this point, they separate until the following season, when they will meet again and mate.

FROM THE CONTINENTAL SHELF TO THE DEEP-SEA WORLD

From a geologic standpoint, the continents of the world are much different from the ocean bottom. The continents have much thicker plates of the earth's solid crust. These plates float on top of a layer of semimolten rock called the "upper mantle." Scientists have determined that the mantle beneath the continents is about 22 miles (35 km) deep. By comparison, the mantle is only 6 miles (10 km) deep beneath the ocean bottom.

Continental Shelves, Slopes, and Ocean Bottoms

The continents are actually dense masses of the earth's crust. The edges of the continents lie below the water's surface, although they are still higher in elevation than the ocean bottoms. The edges are made up of two thin bands. The first is the submerged continental shelf, which represents the crust's border. The second is the continental slope, which is the edge of the continent next to the shelf.

Ten thousand years ago, the continental shelf was largely exposed. At this time, most of the ocean waters were still frozen in the huge continental glaciers of the last ice age. Today, it extends from the low-tide line to a depth of 590 to 656 feet (180 to 200 m). This is the only underwater area that receives light from the sun.

A steep slope falls away from the far edge of the shelf. This area is the continental slope, which leads from the continent's edge to the ocean bottom. The continental slope coincides with the ocean bottom at depths ranging from about 656 feet (200 m) down to about 16,404 feet (5,000 m).

The shelf and the ocean bottom have two completely different environments. The shelf has light and is inhabited by a great variety of life forms. The ocean bottom is dark, mysterious, lacking in plant life, low in oxygen, and under a tremendous amount of water pressure. More information is known about the continental shelf and the areas close to the ocean's surface than about the ocean bottom. The continental shelf and surface waters are affected by sunlight and seasonal changes in temperature. To a certain extent, life in this band is similar to life on land. The depths of the ocean bottom and the lowest zones of the continental slope have more or less uniform conditions at any latitude. They have been explored only in the last few decades.

Life on the Continental Shelf

The continental shelf contains the most typical and varied environments of the ocean. Its climatic and envi-

Opposite page: The only area in the sea that receives the light of the sun is the continental shelf. It extends to a depth of 600 to 650 feet (180 to 200 m) along the edges of the continents. Here, in the shallowest and clearest water, one can find living organisms with many different shapes and colors. An example is the clownfish shown in the photograph.

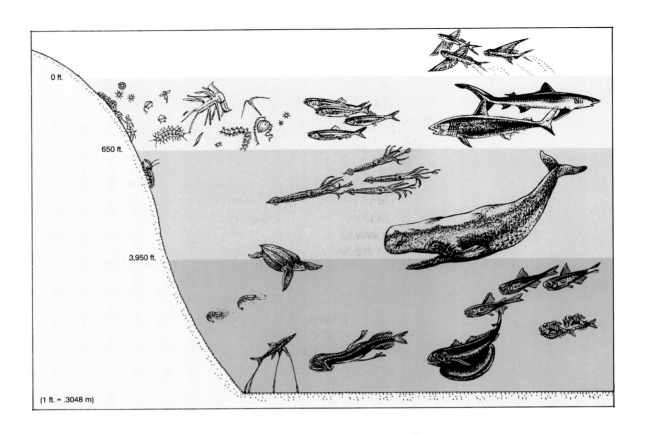

(1 ft. = .3048 m)

Different organisms live at various depths of the ocean. Algae and the tiny animal organisms that eat them are found in the first 656 feet (200 m). Sunlight can reach this zone. Some of the open-sea fish of this zone are the flying fish, herrings, and sharks. Below this is an intermediate zone that partially corresponds to the continental slope. Many organisms that live here come from the zone above it in search of food. Among these are the leatherback sea turtle and the sperm whale. They come to the zone in search of giant cuttlefish. The lowest zone is inhabited by fish and crustaceans.

ronmental features support a great variety of life forms. It also offers many different ecological niches.

More than a million species of animals have been classified on earth. Of these, 80 percent live above water, and only 20 percent live in the sea. However, if insects, which number at least 750,000 species, are excluded from this calculation, the percentage of animals that live in the ocean would be greater. In fact, not counting the insects, two-thirds of the earth's animals are found in salt water, and only one-third are found on land and in fresh water.

All forms of life originally came from the sea. About 90 percent of the basic animal types have ocean relatives. Almost 40 percent of them exist only in the sea. Of the vertebrates, only the amphibians lack an oceanic form. Many mammals, birds, and reptiles have returned to the sea. Most of the more than twenty thousand species of the bony fish live in a saltwater environment. All of the cartilaginous fish, or fish with skeletons consisting mostly of cartilage, live in this environment also. This includes about six hundred species.

Many different organisms inhabit the continental shelf. In this photograph, a carnivorous snail is attacking a jellyfish.

The schools of fish found on the continental shelf are especially complex and interesting. They can be easily divided into two large groups. The first group, consisting of the open-sea fish, is always found near the surface or above certain depths. The second group consists of benthonic fish. These fish live on the bottom or very close to it. These two contrasting environments have led to great differences in the appearance of these fish.

The fish of the open sea, including those of the waters of the continental shelf, are especially adapted for swimming. They do not have many other interesting physical adaptations. Often they are extraordinarily social. They swim in enormous schools that may number in the millions of fish. This is particularly important for commercial fishing.

Many different environments are found at the lowest edge of the continental shelf. Numerous species inhabit this zone, each one represented by a relatively small number of individuals. The greatest number of forms is found on the rocky and coralline parts of the shelf. The species that live in this zone often have extremely unusual shapes, colors, and behavior.

The environment changes as one gets farther from the

continental shelf and descends deeper and deeper into the trenches. The lack of light and heat from the sun allows for few differences among the life forms that live there. At these depths, the type of material composing the bottom is no longer very important. The bottom is simply covered with muddy sediment that originated from flood water or volcanic activity.

In the Pacific Ocean, there are vast expanses located at depths of over 9,842 feet (3,000 m). There are also extremely deep oceanic trenches in the Pacific. The deepest ones are located near Japan, the Philippines, and the Mariana Islands.

The Animals of the Abyss

The deep-sea animals are adapted to a unique environment that completely lacks plant life. It was thought that no life could survive the extreme chemical and physical conditions that are found at the ocean bottom. Recently, however, research has proven otherwise.

There is total darkness at depths below 1,312 feet (400 m). Photosynthesis, the process by which plants use sunlight to produce food from carbon dioxide, water, and minerals, is not possible in these deep waters. No plants can survive under these conditions. Obviously the lack of plant life also reduces the number of animal communities. For food, nonpredatory species must rely on dead plant remains that reach the bottom when they sink from the zones above.

The animals in the deep sea must also be able to survive with very little oxygen. In some oceanic trenches, there is no oxygen at all. The only animals that survive in the trenches are certain species of anaerobic bacteria. Anaerobic organisms are those that can live without oxygen and use other chemical substances to produce energy.

The temperature also rapidly decreases at these depths, reaching a low of 39°F (4°C). Water has a maximum density at this temperature. Under these conditions, the marine animals require more energy when compared to the energy that would be used in surface waters. As a result, animals in the deep are considerably less active. An increase in depth is accompanied by an increase in pressure. The extreme pressure of the deep waters requires the animals living there to develop special adaptations. Because of this development, these organisms are limited to life at certain depths. They cannot survive above such depths.

The giant cuttlefish is an example of this, although it does not possess highly specialized adaptations to the deep waters. The giant cuttlefish actually represents different species of the genus *Architeuthis*. These animals are 60 feet (18 m) long and weigh 551 pounds (250 kg). They inhabit very deep zones of 3,281 feet (1,000 m) and deeper. The few times that they have been observed near the surface, they appeared to be in terrible physical condition.

In 1982, a Norwegian zoologist, Ole Brix, managed to take a blood sample from cuttlefish that had been captured near the surface. He later analyzed the blood sample in his laboratory. He found that the amount of oxygen linked to the hemoglobin (the protein of red blood cells) of the giant cuttlefish decreased four times between temperatures of

43° and 59°F (6° to 15°C). This indicates that these animals may actually suffocate from too much oxygen in shallower and warmer waters. Similarly, they can suffocate if they are caught in a warmer sea current.

In general, the animal life of the deep waters has evolved in relatively recent times. These animals probably developed over the last few million years as they gradually swam in deeper and deeper water. However, there are also more ancient animals at these depths. A mollusk with a conical shell was discovered off the west coast of Mexico at depths below 9,842 feet (3,000 m). The group that these mollusks belong to was thought to have been extinct.

Animal life is less abundant in the deep waters than on the continental shelf. Nevertheless, numerous species of animals inhabit the deep waters. Some of these, like the sea iris, the sea pen, and some sea anemones, have a single stalklike appendage that enables them to move on the muddy bottom. These species fill the bottom half of their bodies with sand or mud in order to anchor themselves to the ocean floor. Certain species of sponges and barnacles are also found at these depths.

Given the absence of plants and plant-eating animals, the food chain has only two levels here. The first is the group of animals that feeds on debris and waste. The second group consists of predators. The sea cucumbers and the sea urchins are part of the first group. They eat enormous quantities of sediment from which they extract nutrients. They then expel the sediment, just as earthworms expel soil after extracting its nutrients. There are also many starfish along with some serpent stars of the *Amphiura* genus. All of them have an extraordinarily slow metabolism. This enables them to survive with very small amounts of food.

In environments of dense water lacking currents and waves, the animals' movements have been reduced to a minimum. These movements are slow and wavelike. Accordingly, the animals gradually developed organs adapted to the scarcity of food. These organs assure the animal of a high level of predatory efficiency and enable it to swallow large pieces of food at once. Many species have enormous mouths and greatly expandable stomachs. Others have skinfolds or protrusions of various types that have a sense of touch. An example of this is the *Linephryne arborifera*, which is just 6 inches (15 cm) long. It has a series of branch-

Sea cucumbers, as seen here, and starfish both belong to the same phylum (Echinodermata). Unlike the starfish, though, most sea cucumbers are not predators. They eat by filtering great quantities of water, from which they extract all types of organic wastes.

Some typical fish of the deep waters are illustrated. *At the upper left* is *Chauilodus sloanei,* with a characteristic long body and a mouth full of sharp teeth. *Below* that is *Melanocetus johnsoni,* with its enormous expandable stomach that can hold large prey. On its head is an appendage that functions as bait. *Center, from the top:* a frogfish, which usually stays on the bottom, attracts prey with its long, luminous filaments. *Bottom:* three examples of hatchet fish and a *Linophryne arborifera,* with its incredible branched appendages, are seen. *Upper right:* a large king eel swims with five types of lantern fish. *Lower right:* a fierce carnivore, *Photostomias quernei,* is pictured.

ing tufts under its "chin" that makes it look like a tiny bush.

Bioluminescence

One of the most surprising adaptations of many animal species of the deep is their ability to produce "cold" light similar to that which common fireflies produce. This phenomenon is common among organisms of the deep waters. Microorganisms, jellyfish, worms, octopuses, squid, shellfish, sea squirts, and certain fish all have this ability. It is also found in land animals. Insects and even some plants like mushrooms and bacteria can also produce this cold light.

These organisms are able to emit light due to a particular chemical substance called "luciferin." This substance produces a chemical reaction that is 100 percent "energy efficient." The existence of luminescent (light-giving) bacteria suggests that this phenomenon may be billions of years old. Since the luciferin system requires oxygen, it is possible that bioluminescence first appeared as an end product of the chemical reactions of very ancient bacteria. These reactions became necessary for the bacteria to survive in the presence of oxygen. Green plants had begun releasing oxygen through the process of photosynthesis. Since oxygen was highly toxic to these bacteria, they developed a series of

chemical reactions to survive. The bacteria continued to produce these chemical reactions even after they were no longer necessary for survival.

A good example of this phenomenon is the single-celled organism *noctiluca scintillans*. This animal emits light when it is disturbed by moving water. Spectacular sights are created at night in waters that are rich with these organisms. Even the movement of a rowboat's oars in these waters causes the organisms to light up.

Various types of shellfish, squids, octopuses, and fish use bioluminescence for hunting other animals. Some deep-water fish are actually equipped with bioluminescent cells at the ends of special appendages or limbs. For example, the *Ceratias halbaelli* has a luminous appendage in front of its mouth that acts as bait. The lantern fish has luminescent cells on the sides of its body. One species of hatchet fish commonly found in the depths of the Pacific Ocean is characterized by luminescent cells and telescopic eyes that are aimed upward. The bodies of all species of hatchet fish are covered with silver plates that reflect the light they emit.

The fish of the *Pachystomias* genus has a particularly elaborate technique for emitting light. This animal's luminescence enables it to prey upon other organisms. The *Pachystomias* fish is able to produce orange or red lights through special "filters." The fish uses these red and orange lights to locate its prey in the dark. Since most deep-water animals are not able to perceive orange and red light, they are unaware of the danger that awaits them. However, because of special pigments in its eye, the *Pachystomias* fish is able to see these lights.

Bioluminescence can also be a disadvantage to a predator. The light produced by a predator may make it visible to another predator. Light cells on the underside of the body are very helpful. They allow the predator to see potential prey beneath it, while preventing it from being seen by other predators above it. The only organisms that cannot use light cells on the underside are those that live on the ocean bottom, like the fishing frog. If they use bioluminescence, they risk being preyed upon by other animals.

GUIDE TO AREAS OF NATURAL INTEREST

The majority of the Pacific islands have a mild climate for most of the year. There are almost no infectious diseases or parasites, and there is a wide variety of food, beautiful scenery, and hospitable people. For many people, though, a trip to the islands remains an impossible dream. They are far away, and it is expensive to reach them.

Tourism in the Pacific islands has grown in recent years, although it is especially rare for Europeans or Americans to visit these islands for the sole purpose of observing nature. Sometimes the islands are a brief stop on a very long trip. Even so, a well-organized person might be able to see much in a short time.

For people with very specific interests, it is best to organize a special trip, keeping in mind that prices may be prohibitive in some areas. Regardless of the cost, the most popular places are often booked well in advance. It may be necessary to make reservations many months in advance to be sure of a place to stay.

New Zealand is different. Because of its "border" position, it is hard to reach unless one has specifically chosen it as a destination. This region offers beautiful natural wonders and a modern, well-organized tourist industry. This enables one to move about easily and to organize a trip based on whatever economic resources are available.

Visiting New Zealand and other points in the Pacific does not require any special equipment or precautions. In some locations, sharks and poisonous sea snakes may be present, although they generally do not bother humans.

When visiting New Zealand, one should be equipped for traveling in the mountains. In the other parts of the Pacific, no special equipment other than binoculars and a camera is needed. To take advantage of the few hours between flights, it is best to travel by rental car or by boat.

An interesting way to visit the ocean is by taking a ship that travels from the west coast of America to Japan or New Zealand. Traveling by ship makes it possible to observe many interesting marine birds like the albatrosses, boobies, tropic birds, and white terns.

Opposite page: A large reef in Micronesia stands covered with vegetation. Its base has been eroded by the action of the sea. A trip through the Pacific islands requires a lot of time and resources. But there is no place in the world that offers such a great opportunity to see nature at its best.

NEW ZEALAND

The parks of New Zealand total more than 7,720 sq. miles (20,000 sq. km) in area. They offer magnificent scenery, including mountains, glaciers, lakes, rivers, fiords, and beaches. The parks are good places to see the interesting plants and animals of this remote part of the world.

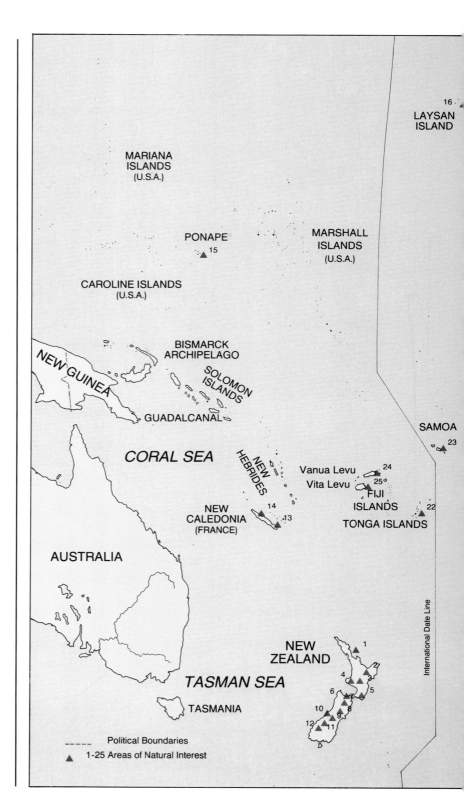

Various small and large islands are scattered throughout the Pacific Ocean. They are far from all the continents. Up until a few years ago, these islands were out of the reach of most European tourists. But the increase in tourism on the islands has recently made this paradise easier to reach.

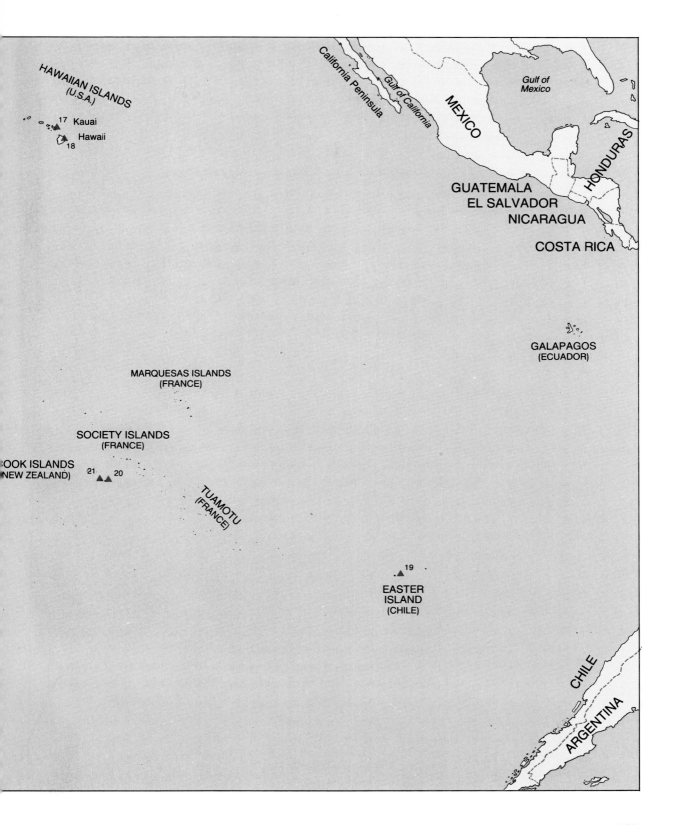

HAWAIIAN ISLANDS
(U.S.A.)

17 Kauai

Hawaii
18

California Peninsula

Gulf of California

MEXICO

Gulf of Mexico

GUATEMALA
EL SALVADOR
NICARAGUA

HONDURAS

COSTA RICA

GALAPAGOS
(ECUADOR)

MARQUESAS ISLANDS
(FRANCE)

SOCIETY ISLANDS
(FRANCE)

COOK ISLANDS
(NEW ZEALAND)

21 20

TUAMOTU
(FRANCE)

19

EASTER
ISLAND
(CHILE)

CHILE

ARGENTINA

Little Barrier (1)

_____

This is a small volcanic island covered by forests. It is located 50 miles (80 km) north of Auckland and can be reached by boat or hydrofoil. The tuatara reptiles are the main attraction of this island. Many other native animals, such as a honey-eating bird unique to Little Barrier, can also be seen here. Other birds on this island include the brown kiwi, the kaka, the brown teal, the white head, and various marine birds.

An unusual species of earthworm is found on Little Barrier. It can reach a length of 55 inches (140 cm).

Urewera (2)

_____

This national park is located in the eastern part of the North Island. It covers about 1 sq. mile (2.6 sq. km). The park is made up of beautiful forests rich with native species of trees, tree ferns, and many lakes, among which are Waikaremoana and Waikare Iti.

The kaka, tuis, Morepork owl, New Zealand parrots, and kiwi are among the best-known birds found here. The deer population of the island is kept within limits by grazing and hunting. The park can be reached by car or bus from Rotorua or Wairoa. Various cabins managed by the forest service are available to visitors.

Tongariro (3)

_____

This was the first national park of New Zealand. It was established in 1894 on land donated by the Maori Chief Te Heuheu Tukino. It is located in the center of the North Island. It extends over 250 sq. miles (650 sq. km) capped with three volcanoes: Ruapehu, Ngauruhoe, and Tongariro. All three are active volcanoes.

Egmont (4)

_____

The province of Taranaki, in the eastern part of the North Island, is dominated by the nearly perfect cone of Mount Egmont. This is an inactive volcano with an elevation of about 8,858 feet (2,700 m). The volcano, together with 116 sq. miles (300 sq. km) of native forest that surround it, makes up a magnificent national park and is a paradise for people who love the mountains.

Among the many native birds of the area are the kiwi, hedge wren, bell bird, and tiny titipounami. Among the nonnative mammals are wild goats and opossum.

Mount Bruce (5)

_____

This bird reserve is about 75 miles (120 km) from Wellington. It is located in the province of Wairarapa in a secondary native forest zone. The takahe, weka, kakapo, blue and brown geese, saddleback, kiwi, and other birds can be seen. This reserve can be visited during weekdays, except during the mating season (October to December).

Abel Tasman (6)

Extending over 69 sq. miles (180 sq. km), this national park runs along the coast in the northern part of South Island. It is especially interesting because it contains a unique mixture of the plant life of the two islands.

The area is also important from an historical point of view, since it was here that the Dutch explorer Abel Tasman landed in 1642.

Nelson Lakes (7)

Surrounded by forests of antarctic beeches, the lakes of Rotoiti and Rotoroa make up a national park that offers splendid scenery and many natural attractions. The lakes can be reached by car or bus from Nelson or Blenheim. Near the lakes are hotels, campgrounds, mountain shelters, and cabins.

Arthur's Pass (8)

This is a national park of 386 sq. miles (1,000 sq. km) on both sides of the most important pass of the Southern Alps of New Zealand. It contains antarctic beech tree forests, rivers, and rain forests at the lower elevations. The famous "wilderness zone of Otehake," one of the most beautiful wild areas of New Zealand, is located in this park.

Kea and kiwi can be seen here, as well as numerous nonnative mammals like the deer and the chamois.

The park can be reached by train from Christchurch, Gremouth, or Hotitika. It can also be reached by car along Interstate Highway 73.

Mount Cook (9)

This national park includes the Cook, Malte Brun, and Liebig mountain chains, which have many peaks and glaciers. The park covers about 270 sq. miles (700 sq. km). Its highest elevation is over 13,000 feet (4,000 m). The Tasman Glacier, which is about 18 miles (29 km) long, is larger than any glaciers of the European Alps. The Aletsch Glacier in Europe, for example, is only about 14 miles (22 km) long. Only the great glaciers of the Himalayan and polar regions are larger than the Tasman Glacier.

Besides the native birds here, there are many nonnative mammals like the chamois, the Himalayan tahr, and the deer, all of which can be hunted.

The park can be reached by car or bus from Christchurch, Timaru, or Oamaru. It is equipped with many hotels, mountain lodges, and campgrounds.

Westland (10)

Mount Aspiring (11)

Fiordland (12)

NEW CALEDONIA

Hauté-Yaté (13)

Ranging in elevation from sea level to over 13,000 feet (4,000 m) above sea level, this park includes sandy and rocky beaches on the Tasman Sea, forests, meadows, waterfalls, lakes, and majestic glaciers. It is located next to Mount Cook Park and represents the natural continuation of the park to the west.

New Zealand pigeons, tuis, Australian herriers, white herons, kotuku, and the bellbirds can be found here. The mammals include the common deer and chamois imported from Europe.

The area can be reached by car or bus from Hokitika or Wanaka through the Lake Wanaka area and the Haast Pass Highway.

Mount Aspiring is known as the "Matterhorn of New Zealand." This nickname is derived from its toothlike form (similar to that of the Matterhorn) and its elevation of 10,827 feet (3,300 m). A national park has been established around this picturesque mountain. The park covers about 770 sq. miles (2,000 sq. km) and includes rivers, forests, valleys, and other beautiful landscapes.

The area can be reached through Queenstown or Wanaka and is equipped with hotels, lodges, and so on.

This is one of the greatest national parks of the world as well as the largest wilderness area in New Zealand. It covers an area of more than 4,632 sq. miles (12,000 sq. km) at the southwest edge of South Island. The last remaining kakapos, takahe, and many other birds are found here. Unfortunately, the large population of imported deer causes many problems for the native species.

The Milford Track is a trail about 31 miles (50 km) long that begins near Lake Te Anau and ends at Milford Sound, crossing some of the most beautiful areas of the park.

The area can be reached by car or bus from Dunedine, Invercargill, or Queenstown, and is well-equipped with hotels, hostels, cabins, and shelters.

This island of French-speaking people located halfway between Brisbane and Fiji is 249 miles (400 km) long and 31 miles (50 km) wide. Many special plants and animals, such as native pigeons, parrots, and sea snakes, are found here.

This reserve is made up of an area covered by tropical

A river of lava flows from Mauna Loa in the Hawaiian Islands. The temperature of the rock can easily exceed 1,832°F (1,000°C) and has actually been measured at almost 2,093°F (1,145°C). The speed of the lava flow is about 12 miles (20 km) an hour.

112

forests. It is located 53 miles (85 km) east of Nouméa, the capital of the island, from which it can be reached by car. Hauté Yaté's forests are home to many palms and native birds like the fruit-eating pigeons and the crested parrot.

Some features of the native forest of New Caledonia have remained almost intact near the city of Nouméa, on Mount Koghis. This mountain can be reached via a road off from the main road that connects Nouméa with the airport.

Mount Koghis (14)

The small hotel of Mount Koghis is located right in the center of the reserve among the forest-dominated mountains. The forests are populated by many interesting birds, such as the New Zealand parrot, the fruit-eating pigeon, two different species of butcher birds, cuckoos, two fan-tailed flycatchers, and others. The kagu is one of the unique birds here, assuming that it still exists. This large bird is native to New Caledonia, although it is very rare in the wild today.

THE CAROLINE ISLANDS

This archipelago is made up of 470 islands whose area totals about 460 sq. miles (1,196 sq. km). The archipelago is located at about 10 degrees latitude north and 130 degrees longitude west and has a semicircular form. The Caroline Islands are among the most beautiful and untouched islands of Micronesia.

Ponape (15)

The island of Ponape is covered by a lush forest crossed by brooks that descend to coasts surrounded by coral reefs. There are also beautiful beaches on the islands of Osakura, Uman, Dublon, Udat, and Tol.

Kusaie is similar to Ponape, from which it can be reached only by boat. For the time being, Kusaie is suited only for travelers with no time limitations.

THE HAWAIIAN ISLANDS

These islands today are much different from their original state, but many natural riches can still be seen here. They are located in the heart of the Pacific Ocean.

Leeward (16)

Uninhabited except for the two most distant atolls (Midway and Kure), these small minor islands of the Hawaiian archipelago are covered only with rocks, coral ruins, and scattered shrubs. They are protected as national animal preserves. They are especially important for marine birds, which have no other suitable nesting ground in the

North Pacific.

The entire land area of this chain of atolls, which stretches 746 miles (1,200 km) from Kauai to Kure, is only 12 sq. miles (30 sq. km). Even so, more than three million albatrosses are found there. Eighty percent of them are Layan albabrosses. Today, there is an American military base and an airport on Midway.

Hawaii Volcanoes National Park (17)

This national park rises from sea level to 13,681 feet (4,170 m) and includes the craters of the Kilauea and Mauna Loa volcanoes. The park covers almost 340 sq. miles (880 sq. km) in the southeast part of the island of Hawaii. The area is partly covered by tropical forests of ohia, persimmon, koa acacias, and tree ferns. There are a few shrubby areas and meadows where native species such as *Deschampsia australis* grow.

The fauna includes the famous black goose, the Hawaiian buzzard, the Hawaiian crow, and many other birds such as the akepa, akiapolaau, ou, elepaio, and iwi.

Kauai (18)

The green, mountainous island of Kauai, northwest of Oahu, is known as an island garden. Two roads run along its coasts. One runs in a southwesterly direction that reaches the Hanapepe Valley, the Waimea Canyon, and Kokee State Park. The other runs toward the north and stops at the Kilauea lighthouse. Hanapepe and Waimea are noted for their rich vegetation. Kokee Park is a virgin forest of ohialehua trees with ferns, lichens, mosses, and many native and nonnative birds.

Kilauea, finally, is noted for its colony of red-footed boobies, which can be seen close-up, near their nests.

CHILE

Easter Island (19)

Easter Island is among the easternmost of the Polynesian Islands. It covers 46 sq. miles (118 sq. km) and is located at about 27 degrees latitude south and 109 degrees longitude west. It can easily be reached today since it is a regular stop on flights between Tahiti and Santiago de Chile. The island has been a part of Chile since 1888. Easter Island is about 2,330 miles (3,750 km) off the west coast of Chile.

Easter Island is especially interesting for its splendid volcanic scenery, the coasts, and the caves, but it is most famous for the huge monuments carved out of volcanic rock. They average 10 to 16 feet (3 to 5 m) tall, but some are as tall as 33 feet (10 m).

The hot springs of Rotorua in New Zealand are similar to geysers. The underground molten rock heats the water in faults. The water then shoots up like a geyser or rises slowly in the form of vapor.

THE SOCIETY ISLANDS

Tahiti (20)

Moorea (21)

THE TONGA ISLANDS

Tangatapu, Ha'apai, and Vava'u (22)

Located south of the equator, these islands extend over 636 sq. miles (1,647 sq. km). Together with the Marquesas, Austral (or Tubuai), and Tuamotu islands, they make up French Polynesia, which includes a large number of tiny little islands and atolls for a total area of 1,544 sq. miles (4,000 sq. km).

Tahiti is characterized by high volcanic peaks hidden by dense vegetation of tree ferns, wild bananas, and Tahitian chestnuts. This dense plant life makes the interior almost impassable. The island is surrounded by a coral reef that encircles beautiful, calm lagoons. Lake Vahiria, the only volcanic lake of Polynesia, is 1,640 feet (500 m) above sea level and is located high up on the volcanic peaks.

Tahiti is considered the most romantic island of Polynesia. Besides the botanical park with its memorial museum to the French artist Paul Gauguin, there is also an interesting underwater marine aquarium. It is possible to cross the entire island on foot from north to south, climbing from the Papenoo Valley to Lake Vahiria and descending through the Mataiea Valley.

This island can be reached from Tahiti daily by sea or air. A splendid lagoon bordered with coconut palms and fantastic pinnacles of lava rock is found here. Tropical birds and white terns nest along its coastlines.

Of equal beauty and interest are Bora-Bora, Huahine, Raiatea, Tahaa, and Maupiti.

Nicknamed the "Friendly Islands," by the explorer James Cook, the Tonga archipelago is still one of the most hospitable lands in the world. This archipelago includes 170 islands covering a total area of 270 sq. miles (700 sq. km).

The island of Tangatapu, where the capital city of Nuku'alofa is located, can be reached by air from New Zealand, the Samoan Islands, Fiji, and the Cook Islands. White beaches in a tropical ocean atmosphere are common here. During the day, bats rest by the thousands in trees near Kolevai. Other special attractions are the blowholes (high jets of water pushed through narrow crevices of rocks by ocean waves) and the nearby islands of Ha'apai and Vava'u, with their beautiful beaches and traditional Pacific atmosphere.

THE SAMOAN ISLANDS

The Samoan Islands are divided into an eastern and a western group. They are located from 280 to 500 miles (450 to 800 km) northeast of Fiji. To naturalists, they are especially important because of their interesting native doves, including the one that resembles the now-extinct dodo bird of the island of Mauritius. This bird has a powerful curved beak similar to that of a bird of prey.

Le Pupu Pue (23)

This park consists of a large lava bed populated by swallows and bats. It covers 10 sq. miles (25 sq. km) of western Samoa. The park is surrounded by tropical forests that form at least ten different plant communities. Fifty species of birds, reptiles, and mammals are found in the park. At least twenty-one of these are native to Samoa, and ten are rare or endangered species.

THE FIJI ISLANDS

The Fiji Islands are an important stop for people traveling across the Pacific by air. Despite the fact that they appear very tiny in the great expanse of the ocean, the two main islands are rather large. Viti Levu is 90 miles (145 km) long and 60 miles (96 km) wide. Vanua Levu is 104 miles (168 km) long and 30 miles (48 km) wide. Visitors to these islands can see animal life that has no comparison in any other part of the world.

Vanua Levu (24)

This beautiful island can be reached by air from Viti Levu. It is home to many birds, the most memorable of which are the beautiful orange fruit-eating pigeon and the unusual silktail.

The little island of Taveuni, located near the eastern coast of Vanua Levu, is covered with a tropical forest rich with many species of exotic and beautiful birds. This island is also ideal for snorkeling.

Viti Levu (25)

The center of the island can be reached by renting a car at the Nadi airport (on the western side of the island). There in the Nausori Highlands, a beautiful tropical forest still exists. Various species of doves and fruit-eating pigeons, ringed lorikeets, musky parrots, Polynesian starlings, and many other species are abundant in this forest.

Another interesting place is the botanical garden of Suva, the capital of the island, which is located on the eastern coast. Many native and nonnative birds as well as plants can be seen here.

Following pages: Blowholes are seen on the southwest coast of Tongatapu on the island of Tonga.

GLOSSARY

adaptation change or adjustment by which a species or individual improves its condition in relationship to its environment.

algae primitive organisms which resemble plants but do not have true roots, stems, or leaves.

amphibian any of a class of vertebrates that usually begins life in the water as a tadpole with gills and later develops lungs.

archaeology the scientific study of the life and culture of ancient peoples.

archipelago a group or chain of many islands.

atmosphere the gaseous mass surrounding the earth. The atmosphere consists of oxygen, nitrogen, and other gases, and extends to a height of 22,000 miles (35,000 kilometers).

benthos all the plants and animals living on or closely associated with the bottom of a body of water, especially the ocean.

biogeography the branch of biology that deals with the geographical distribution of plants and animals.

biology the science that deals with the origin, history, physical characteristics, and life processes of living things.

bioluminescence the production of light by living organisms such as fireflies.

conservation the controlled use and systematic protection of natural resources, such as forests and waterways.

continent one of the principal land masses of the earth. Africa, Antarctica, Asia, Europe, North America, South America, and Australia are regarded as continents.

ecology the relationship between organisms and their environment.

environment the circumstances or conditions of a plant or animal's surroundings.

erosion natural processes such as weathering, abrasion, and corrosion, by which material is removed from the earth's surface.

evolution a gradual process in which something changes into a different and usually more complex or better form.

extinction the process of destroying or extinguishing.

fault a fracture or split in a rock mass, accompanied by movement of one part along the split.

fauna the animals of a particular region or period.

fiord a narrow inlet or arm of the sea bordered by steep cliffs.

fossil a remnant or trace of an organism of a past geologic age, such as a skeleton or leaf imprint, embedded in some part of the earth's crust.

genus a classification of plants or animals with common distinguishing characteristics. A genus is the main subdivision of a family and is made up of a small group of closely related species or of a single species.

geyser a spring from which columns of boiling water and steam gush into the air at intervals.

glaciers gigantic moving sheets of ice that covered great areas of the earth in an earlier time. Glaciers existed primarily in the Pleistocene period, one million years ago.

gorge a deep, narrow pass between steep heights.

habitat the area or type of environment in which a person or other organism normally occurs.

herbivore an animal that eats plants.

hibernate to spend the winter in a dormant state.

humid containing a large amount of water or water vapor.

incubate to keep eggs in a favorable environment for hatching.

invertebrate lacking a backbone or spinal column.

larva the early, immature form of any animal that changes structurally when it becomes an adult.

lichen a primitive plant formed by the association of blue-green algae with fungi.

magma the molten matter under the earth's crust which is eventually released in a volcanic eruption.

mantle the layer of the earth's interior between the crust and the core. The earth's mantle beneath the continents is about 22 miles (35 kilometers) deep.

marsupial an animal that carries and nurses its young in a pouch on the mother's body.

migrate to move from one region to another with the change in seasons. Many animals have steady migration patterns.

naturalist a person who studies nature, especially by direct observation of animals and plants.

niche the specific space occupied by an organism within its habitat; a small space or hollow.

omnivore an animal that eats both plants and other animals.

organism any individual animal or plant having diverse organs and parts that function as a whole to maintain life and its activities.

paleontology the branch of geology that deals with prehistoric forms of life through the study of plant and animals fossils.

parasite an organism that grows, feeds, and is sheltered on or in a different organism while contributing nothing to the survival of its host.

phytoplankton small, floating aquatic plants.

photosynthesis the process by which chlorophyll-containing cells in green plants convert sunlight into chemical energy and change inorganic compounds into organic compounds.

plankton microscopic plant and animal organisms which float or drift in the ocean or in bodies of fresh water.

predator an animal that lives by preying on others. Predators kill other animals for food.

rain forest a dense, evergreen forest occupying a tropical region having abundant rainfall throughout the year.

reptile a cold-blooded vertebrate having lungs, a bony skeleton, and a body covered with scales or horny plates.

rodent any of a very large order of gnawing animals, characterized by constantly growing teeth adapted for chewing or nibbling.

salinity of or relating to the saltiness of something. The salinity of ocean water, for instance, varies in different regions and depths.

savanna a treeless plain or a grassland characterized by scattered trees, especially in tropical or subtropical regions having seasonal rains.

species a distinct kind, sort, variety, or class.

vertebrate having a backbone or spinal column.

zooplankton floating, often microscopic sea animals.

INDEX

CREDITS

MAPS AND DRAWINGS. G. Scarato and F. Spaliviero, Colgna Veneta (VR). **PHOTOGRAPHS. Archivio 2P,** Milan: 42-43, 44, 110. **A. Borroni,** Milan: Mairani 6-7, 40-41, 63. **G. Coato,** Verona: 59. **C. Giacoma,** Torino: 21, 69. **Marka Graphic,** Milan: 30-31; P. Curto 120-121; Dallas & J. Heaton 46; Globe Photos 104; C. Mauri 26-27; N. Myers 64-65. **Overseas,** Milan: M. Macintyre 116-117; J. P. Nacivet 12-13; Explorer/Krafft 112-113; Jacan 76-77; Jacana/Jouve 92-93; Jacana/Laboute 72; Jacana/J. P. Varin-A. Visage 51; Oxford Scientific Films/W. Cheng 67; Oxford Scientific Films/D. A. Curl 70-71; Oxford Scientific Films/Mantis Wildlife Films 81; Oxford Scientific Films R. Packwood 16, 29; Oxford Scientific Films/P. Parks 94, 97; Oxford Scientific Films/C. M. Perrins 48-49; Oxford Scientific Films/D. Renn 91; Oxford Scientific Films/M. Tibbles 87. **Panda Photo,** Rome: Ardea Photo/V. Taylor 98-99; D. Cavagnaro 39; S. Cedola 56-57; C. Consiglio 68; P. Harris 82-83; T. Lilleby 19; New Zealand Wildlife Service 24, 35; A. Petretti-F. Petretti 75; L. Sonnino Sorisio 60-61, 78, 84-85, 100, 101; M. Sonnino Sorisio 62. **L. Pellegrini,** Milan: **L. Ricciarini,** Milan: Archivio 2P sovracoperta. **F. Speranza,** Milan: T. Dawes 88-89. **M.P. Stradella,** Milan: Studio Pizzi 58, G. Ricatto 54-55.